REPORT

The Economics of Air Force Medical Service Readiness

John C. Graser, Daniel Blum, Kevin Brancato,
James J. Burks, Edward W. Chan, Nancy Nicosia,
Michael J. Neumann, Hans V. Ritschard,
Benjamin F. Mundell

Prepared for the United States Air Force

PROJECT AIR FORCE

The research described in this report was sponsored by the United States Air Force under Contract FA7014-06-C-0001. Further information may be obtained from the Strategic Planning Division, Directorate of Plans, Hq USAF.

Library of Congress Cataloging-in-Publication Data

The economics of Air Force Medical Service readiness / John C. Graser ... [et al.].
    p. cm.
  Includes bibliographical references.
  ISBN 978-0-8330-5022-9 (pbk. : alk. paper)
  1. United States. Air Force Medical Service—Evaluation. 2. United States. Air Force Medical Service—
Reorganization. 3. United States. Air Force—Medical care. 4. United States. Air Force—Operational readiness.
I. Graser, John C.

  UG983.E35 2011
  358.4'13450973—dc22

                                                                                          2010047950

The RAND Corporation is a nonprofit institution that helps improve policy and decisionmaking through research and analysis. RAND's publications do not necessarily reflect the opinions of its research clients and sponsors.

RAND® is a registered trademark.

Published 2010 by the RAND Corporation
1776 Main Street, P.O. Box 2138, Santa Monica, CA 90407-2138
1200 South Hayes Street, Arlington, VA 22202-5050
4570 Fifth Avenue, Suite 600, Pittsburgh, PA 15213-2665
RAND URL: http://www.rand.org/
To order RAND documents or to obtain additional information, contact
Distribution Services: Telephone: (310) 451-7002;
Fax: (310) 451-6915; Email: order@rand.org

Preface

The Air Force Medical Service (AFMS) has three major missions: keeping the Air Force active-duty population healthy and deployable for their wartime mission; maintaining the readiness of AFMS personnel to perform their wartime health-care mission; and providing health-care services for Air Force and other Department of Defense (DoD) retirees, dependents, and other categories of eligible beneficiaries. To accomplish these missions, AFMS has a full-time force of about 40,000 military and civilian personnel who operate 74 military treatment facilities (MTFs) throughout the world and provide health care to about 2.6 million eligible beneficiaries. In addition, the Air National Guard and Air Force Reserve have about 20,000 medical personnel.

Since 2001, as part of the global war on terror, AFMS and the medical departments of the Army and Navy have been tasked with supporting combat operations in Afghanistan and Iraq. Specialists providing critical care, specifically surgeons and operating room nurses and technicians, as well as mental health professionals, have been in high demand. In addition to the problem of filling these in-theater requirements with highly trained specialists, deployments present another problem to AFMS: how to provide for the home-station health care these specialists would normally accomplish if they were not deployed. Their absence means that some beneficiaries must find alternative sources of medical care. In addition, current funding methodologies mean that the resulting decreases in workloads (number of medical procedures performed) at the home station can adversely affect the portions of the AFMS budget that depend on these workloads to generate that funding. A final complication in the AFMS operating environment is the reduction in the number of inpatient facilities and overall inpatient workload, which has decreased opportunities for training critical-care specialists for wartime duties.

Under a project entitled "Economics of Air Force Medical Service Readiness," the project sponsor, then–Deputy Surgeon of the Air Force, Maj Gen C. Bruce Green, asked RAND Project AIR FORCE to assess the AFMS operation by

- evaluating how AFMS functions as a health plan, a health-care provider, and a payer for services, as well as how it relates to other DoD organizations
- examining how resource decisions are made and how the Medical Expense and Performance Reporting System and other systems and processes affect resource allocation within the U.S. Military Health System
- analyzing the effects of resource decisions on system incentives and medical readiness
- examining alternative methodologies for solving problems that are discovered.

The research was conducted within the Resource Management Program of RAND Project AIR FORCE. Data collection and analysis were performed between January 2008 and September 2008, and a final project update was provided to the sponsor in September 2008, with frequent updates in between.

This report should be of interest to government personnel with a stake in military healthcare operations and resourcing issues. Related documents include the following:

- Christine Eibner, *Maintaining Military Medical Skills During Peacetime: Outlining and Assessing a New Approach*, Santa Monica, Calif.: RAND Corporation, MG-638-OSD, 2008.
- Edward G. Keating, Marygail K. Brauner, Lionel A. Galway, Judith D. Mele, James J. Burks, and Brendan Saloner, *Air Force Physician and Dentist Multiyear Special Pay: Current Status and Potential Reforms*, Santa Monica, Calif.: RAND Corporation, MG-866-AF, 2009.
- Edward G. Keating, Hugh G. Massey, Judith D. Mele, and Benjamin F. Mundell, *An Analysis of the Populations of the Air Force's Medical and Professional Officer Corps*, Santa Monica, Calif.: RAND Corporation, TR-782-AF, 2010.
- Don Snyder, Edward W. Chan, James J. Burks, Mahyar A. Amouzegar, and Adam C. Resnick, *How Should Air Force Expeditionary Medical Capabilities Be Expressed?* Santa Monica, Calif.: RAND Corporation, MG-785-AF, 2009.

RAND Project AIR FORCE

RAND Project AIR FORCE (PAF), a division of the RAND Corporation, is the U.S. Air Force's federally funded research and development center for studies and analyses. PAF provides the Air Force with independent analyses of policy alternatives affecting the development, employment, combat readiness, and support of current and future aerospace forces. Research is conducted in four programs: Force Modernization and Employment; Manpower, Personnel, and Training; Resource Management; and Strategy and Doctrine.

Additional information about PAF is available on our website:
http://www.rand.org/paf/

Contents

Figures

Tables

Summary

AFMS is facing a challenging environment. As key providers of medical support for operations Iraqi Freedom and Enduring Freedom, AFMS personnel operate three theater hospitals that provide health care to deployed forces from all four services. Much of this health care is provided to severely injured or wounded U.S. personnel, as well as to civilians in Iraq and Afghanistan. At the same time, they have continued the mission of stabilizing wounded and injured patients and providing expeditious aeromedical evacuation of personnel out of theater.

Although AFMS has been successful in meeting these requirements, the operation of in-theater hospitals is an added responsibility that was not envisioned when the Air Expeditionary Force concept for sizing and training for AFMS deployment capabilities was established in the late 1990s. Under this concept, AFMS was structured to support Air Force units deployed in theater and to provide aeromedical evacuation for all the services.

The care of the severely injured and wounded depends on teams of critical-care specialists, including surgeons, operating room and intensive care nurses, and surgical technicians. To stay ready for wartime and maintain their surgical skills in peacetime, these AFMS teams must operate on patients with a wide variety of health needs. While replicating the severity of combat wounds and injuries in peacetime is difficult, regular surgery at least provides these teams with the surgical experience necessary to maintain their technical proficiency. Also known as *currency opportunities*, assignments that allow the teams to maintain surgical skills in a hospital and surgical environment are referred to as the *inpatient workload* in this report.[1] (See p. 46.)

To scope the currency situation and the ability of the Air Force to function as a provider of medical services and the issues it faces in accomplishing these goals, we interviewed a wide variety of medical and support personnel within AFMS, the Army and Navy medical services, and the Office of the Assistant Secretary of Defense, Health Affairs (OASD[HA]) and gathered data on currency opportunities, workload accomplishments, and funding. Although we found a widespread commitment to providing quality medical care to DoD beneficiaries, we also noted a variety of opinions about how AFMS and other services' medical care systems should address many of the issues they face.

All the services must continue providing superior care to the wounded and injured from combat and normal military operations as a first priority, but they must also provide quality peacetime care to beneficiaries, conduct health-care operations as efficiently as possible, and

---

[1]   We use inpatient workload as a proxy for evaluating overall opportunities to retain surgical currency. Some of the outpatient workload at ambulatory surgical centers (ASCs) could also provide currency opportunities, depending on the particular surgical specialty. However, for severe combat injuries, which require more-invasive surgery, an inpatient stay would align more closely with that currency opportunity.

maintain the currency of their health-care providers. To do this, they must recruit, train, and retain a highly skilled, deployable medical force by providing professional opportunities that help attract high-quality medical personnel. Graduate medical education and military-unique specialized training are critical to accomplishing these goals and supporting medical readiness. Yet all this must happen in the context of the increasing costs of medical care and the focus on reducing forecast cost increases. Our description of these challenges and our recommendations are based in part on these interviews and our analysis of the data provided.

Over the past two decades, AFMS has faced a major reduction in its inpatient workload for a number of reasons. The primary reason has been a decline in the number of AFMS hospitals (where inpatient procedures are performed), from 76 in 1992 to 15 in 2008, a decrease of 80 percent. This contraction was due both to hospital closures (many were shuttered as Air Force bases were closed after the end of the Cold War) and to the conversion of many hospitals into stand-alone clinics or ASCs.

The reasons for converting hospitals to stand-alone clinics and ASCs are complex. In some instances, AFMS elected to convert smaller hospitals because they lacked the workload to keep their surgical teams trained, creating concern about the quality of care they provided. Others were converted because of external decisions, such as a 2005 Base Realignment and Closure direction to convert five AFMS hospitals to clinics or ASCs. (See pp. 8–10.)

In addition to the reduction in the number of facilities capable of inpatient procedures, the AFMS surgical workload, along with those of the Army and Navy medical departments, has decreased because of the passage of the TRICARE for Life legislation, which essentially eliminated any financial incentive for Medicare-eligible DoD beneficiaries to use military hospitals. Previously, these beneficiaries had to pay part of the cost of their care if they elected to use a civilian physician. The decreased workload from this older DoD beneficiary population was significant because it provided a substantial percentage of the inpatient workload critical for surgical teams to maintain readiness. (See pp. 52–54.)

At the same time, OASD(HA), facing rising health-care costs throughout the military community, established budget-allocation processes that linked a portion of the services' funding to their patient workloads. These methodologies were designed as incentives for the military medical departments to maintain or increase their annual workloads or to risk budget reductions. The rationale was that, if DoD was purchasing an increasing proportion of health care from the civilian sector, the service medical departments' should decrease commensurately to account for the decreased workload.

Under this budget-allocation process, the inpatient workload is vital because payments for inpatient work can be more than 150 times higher than for outpatient visits.[2] However, retaining or increasing the inpatient workload is more difficult when surgical teams deploy from MTFs because, under current workload reporting policies and systems, the teams earn no workload credit for procedures they perform elsewhere. So, unless reservists or civilians can be found to fill in for deployed medical personnel, the home MTFs are less able to handle the normal workload. Thus far, the savings in pharmacy costs and additional funds and supplemental appropriations passed annually since fiscal year 2002 for the global war on terror have mitigated the resource implications of this lost workload somewhat. (See pp. 17–32.)

---

[2] This difference is driven primarily by the facility cost portion of the procedures, not the professional services costs.

In addition to the factors described above, AFMS will face some very significant challenges in the future. In response to a 2005 Base Realignment and Closure decision, AFMS's flagship hospital, Wilford Hall Medical Center (WHMC), is being converted into an ASC. WHMC performed more than 40 percent of AFMS's inpatient procedures and was also the only Level I trauma and emergency room referral center in AFMS. The center also served as a training and currency platform for a wide variety of surgical and nonsurgical skills, including training for future AFMS leadership. Although AFMS personnel will continue to perform much of WHMC's surgical work at the new Air Force–Army San Antonio Military Medical Center (SAMMC), the identification and documentation of the AFMS workload may be jeopardized, possibly resulting in the misperception that the workload decreased further, which could affect recruitment or the very existence of AFMS inpatient capabilities. It is also currently unclear how medical resources at SAMMC will be allocated between the U.S. Air Force and U.S. Army. To ensure that AFMS gets both the resources and the recognition for its SAMMC workload, we recommend that the AFMS leadership advocate that OASD(HA) suspend the current workload-based funding methodologies at SAMMC until experience is gained with the new organization. (See pp. 41, 91–97.)

To maintain a cadre of critical-care specialists ready for wartime deployment, AFMS may have to increase its inpatient workload at AFMS hospitals or find alternatives for training critical-care specialists at non-AFMS hospitals. Training alternatives could include assignments to other services' hospitals, partnerships with the U.S. Department of Veterans Affairs hospitals or civilian hospitals, or greater use of Air National Guard or Air Force Reserve medical personnel in wartime. Solutions to these challenges are essential for AFMS to meet its wartime critical-care responsibilities; to ensure proper resourcing under OASD(HA)'s "pay-for-performance" metrics; and to be viewed as a vibrant, viable medical service offering interesting work to potential medical professionals.[3] (See pp. 57–67.)

---

[3] AFMS commissioned a subsequent RAND study to investigate these workload enhancing options further.

Acknowledgments

We would like to thank the many individuals we interviewed as part of this project: OASD(HA), the TRICARE Management Activity, the service headquarters, and Air Force and Army MTFs. The following individuals freely gave their time and information to help us complete this study; their offices and ranks were current as of the time of the research:

Surgeon General of the Air Force and Staff
   Maj Gen C. Bruce Green, M.D.
      Brig Gen Patricia Lewis   Lt Col Dan Lee
      Col Dennis Beatty   Maj Frank Capoccia
      Col Joseph Kennedy   Maj Andi Vinyard
      Col Arnyce Pock   Denise Comfort

Air Force Medical Operating Agency, Arlington, Virginia
      Col JoAnne McPherson   Lt Col Brenda Hanes
      Maj Shawn Bransky   Capt Kevin Bozzi
      Maj Melanie Carino   Darrell Dorian
      Maj Merilyn Jenkins   Avery Smith
      Maj Ted Woolley

Air National Guard Surgeon General
   Col Chip Riggins (and staff)

Former Air Force Surgeons General
      Lt Gen Paul Carlton, M.D. (Ret)   Lt Gen George Taylor, M.D. (Ret)
      Lt Gen Charles Roadman II, M.D. (Ret)

OASD(HA)/TRICARE Medical Agency
      Greg Atkinson   Al Middleton
      Ken Cox   Robert Moss
      Michael Dinneen, M.D.   Robert Opsut, Ph.D.
      Dr. Richard Guerin   Patrick Wesley (and staff)

Office of the Army Surgeon General
      Col Daryl Spencer   Herb Coley
      Ramona Bacon

59th Medical Wing, Lackland AFB, Texas
      Maj Gen Tom Travis (and staff)   Col Robert Hamilton (and staff)

10th Medical Group, Air Force Academy Hospital, Colorado

     Michael Love   Kristy Viera

61st Medical Group, Los Angeles Air Force Base, California

     Robert Donald

89th Medical Wing, Andrews AFB, Maryland

     Maj Gen Gar Graham

Commander, Joint Task Force, National Capital Region Medical

     VADM John Mateczun

Brooke Army Medical Center, Ft. Sam Houston, Texas

     Brig Gen James Gilman (and staff)   Dewey Mitchell

     Col David Bitterman (and staff)

Landstuhl Regional Medical Center, Landstuhl, Germany

     Lt Col Melissa Checotah

Navy Bureau of Medicine and Surgery, Washington, D.C.

     Roma Collinsworth (and staff)   Jane Cunningham

Veterans Health Administration, Washington, D.C.

     BG Michael Kussman, M.D. (USA Ret),   COL Gerald Cross, M.D. (USA Ret),
     Under Secretary, Health   Deputy Under Secretary, Health

We would like to thank Susan Hosek for her help and insights early in the project formulation stage. We would also like to thank our other colleagues at RAND (Ellen Pint and Christine Eibner) and Robert Opsut of the OASD(HA) for their reviews and comments on the draft report. Finally, we would like to thank Laura Baldwin for her thoughtful suggestions throughout the project.

Abbreviations

AB	air base
ACC	ambulatory care center
ACH	Army community hospital
AE	aeromedical evacuation
AEF	Air Expeditionary Force
AF/SG8P	Air Force Surgeon General Programs Division
AFB	Air Force base
AFMOA	Air Force Medical Operations Agency
AFMS	Air Force Medical Service
AHC	Army health clinic
AMC	Army medical center
ASC	ambulatory surgical center
ASD(HA)	Assistant Secretary of Defense for Health Affairs
BAMC	Brooke Army Medical Center
BRAC	Base Realignment and Closure
CBO	Congressional Budget Office
CHAMPUS	Civilian Health and Medical Program of the Uniformed Services
CHCS	Composite Health Care System
CMAC	CHAMPUS Maximum Allowable Charge
COCOM	combatant commander
CONUS	continental United States
CRIS	Commander's Resource Integration System
DHP	Defense Health Program
DMHRSi	Defense Medical Human Resources System–Internet

DMIS	Defense Medical Information System
DoD	Department of Defense
DoDD	Department of Defense Directive
EAS IV	Expense Assignment System IV
EMEDS	emergency medical support
FTE	full-time equivalent
FY	fiscal year
GAO	Government Accountability Office
GME	graduate medical education
GWOT	global war on terror
HQ	headquarters
ISS	injury severity score
LRMC	Landstuhl Regional Medical Center
M2	MHS Management Analysis and Reporting Tool
MAJCOM	major command (Air Force)
MDG	medical group
MDS	medical squadron
MDW	medical wing
MEPRS	Medical Expense and Performance Reporting System
MERHCF	Medicare Eligible Retiree Health Care Fund
MHS	U.S. Military Health System
MILCON	military construction (budget item)
MILPERS	military personnel (budget item)
MTF	military treatment facility
NH	naval hospital
NHC	naval health clinic
NMC	naval medical center
NNMC	national naval medical center
NPI	National Provider Identification
O&M	operation and maintenance (budget item)

OASD(HA)	Office of the Assistant Secretary of Defense, Health Affairs
OSD	Office of the Secretary of Defense
PEC	program element code
POM	program objective memorandum
PPBE	planning, programming, budgeting, and execution
PPS	Prospective Payment System
R&D	research and development (budget item)
RVU	relative value unit
RWP	relative weighted product
SADR	Standard Ambulatory Data Record
SAMMC	San Antonio Military Medical Center
SIDR	Standard Inpatient Data Record
STANFINS	Standard Financial System
STARS-FL	Standard Accounting and Reporting System–Field Level
TFL	TRICARE for Life
TMA	TRICARE Management Activity
USD(P&R)	Under Secretary of Defense for Personnel and Readiness
VA	U.S. Department of Veterans Affairs
VHA	Veterans Health Administration
WHMC	Wilford Hall Medical Center

Glossary

ambulatory care

Any medical care delivered on an outpatient basis is ambulatory. Many medical conditions do not require hospital admission and can be managed without it. Many medical investigations can be performed on an ambulatory basis, including blood tests, X-rays, endoscopy, and even biopsy procedures of superficial organs. Synonymous with ambulatory care workload and outpatient care workload.

ambulatory surgical centers

These medical facilities specialize in elective same-day or outpatient surgical procedures. They do not offer emergency care or have intensive postoperative capabilities. Patients treated in these surgical centers do not require admission to a hospital and are well enough to go home after the procedure.

clinical currency

This is what medical personnel who have received the required training and experience to perform their medical duties without further training, instruction, or experience possess. Thus, a surgeon would be clinically current if he or she were capable of performing surgery in his or her specialty immediately after arrival at a deployment site.

earnings

Compensation provided to the services or individual MTFs based on the performance of either forecast or actual health care procedures. Synonymous with revenue.

inpatient care

Inpatient care refers to medical treatment provided in a hospital or other facility and that requires at least one overnight stay. Not all inpatient care involves surgery, but significant surgery involves inpatient care. Synonymous with inpatient care workload.

medical workload

This term can refer to the requirement for an individual or for aggregate medical procedure(s) or to the performance of an individual or aggregate medical procedure(s).

parent military treatment facility	An MTF that reports workload and expense data under the Medical Expense and Performance Reporting System (MEPRS). Under MEPRS, every medical center, hospital, or dental center that is not a subordinate entity is required to report. If an MTF has subordinate clinics which report to it, their data are consolidated and reported at the parent level. In the Army and Navy, subordinate clinics report their information through their "parent" MTF; AFMS has no subordinate clinics and all AFMS MTFs report their own MEPRS data.
relative value unit	Hospitals use RVUs to compare the amounts of resources required to perform various services within a single department or between departments. It is determined by assigning weight to such factors as personnel time, level of skill, and sophistication of equipment required to render patient services. RVUs are a common method of measuring workload for physician bonus plans based partially on productivity.
relative weighted product	DoD uses RWPs to measure workload that compares the resource consumption of a patient's hospitalization to that of other patients.
stand-alone clinic	This term describes a medical clinic that is not collocated with a hospital.

CHAPTER ONE

Introduction

Background

The immense value of the U.S. Military Health System (MHS) and its modern battlefield techniques for providing initial life-sustaining medical intervention and treatment and rapid aeromedical evacuation (AE) for the critically wounded have been demonstrated during military operations in Iraq and Afghanistan. Survival rates for the seriously wounded are the highest in U.S. military history, as measured by the died-of-wounds rate. In addition, the services have experienced their lowest historical rates for disease and nonbattle injuries.

To provide medical services, each military department runs its own health-care operations as part of the larger MHS, under the policy and fiscal guidance of the Office of the Under Secretary of Defense for Personnel and Readiness (USD[P&R]) and the Office of the Assistant Secretary of Defense for Health Affairs (OASD[HA]). Each military department's medical service is primarily designed to provide care to its own active-duty population in both peacetime and wartime. However, any active-duty member can be treated at any military treatment facility (MTF). In addition, the military medical departments provide care to dependents of active-duty members and to retirees and their dependents.

AFMS, much like the Army and Navy medical departments, has three primary missions:

- maintain a healthy active-duty force
- maintain a trained, ready, and deployable medical force
- provide peacetime health care to dependents and retirees.

The military medical services require a combination of four major, integrated, and balanced inputs (see Figure 1.1): medical facilities, properly trained and ready medical manpower, appropriate funding, and a sufficiently diverse patient population for the staff to maintain its clinical skills. The output of MHF is clinical workload completion, which can be defined as prevention of injury, illness, or disease or intervention to cure injury, illness, or disease when it occurs. This system produces the three primary outcomes (missions) of MHS. Overall military readiness is related to the first two outcomes (highlighted in Figure 1.1).[1] AFMS readiness

---

[1] The following definition of medical readiness applies in this report:

> Medical readiness—encompasses the ability to mobilize, deploy and sustain field medical services and support for any operation requiring military services; to maintain and project the continuum of health-care resources required to provide for the health of the force; and to operate in conjunction with beneficiary healthcare. (DoD, 1995, p. 27)

Figure 1.1
Inputs, Outputs, and Outcomes of the Military Health System

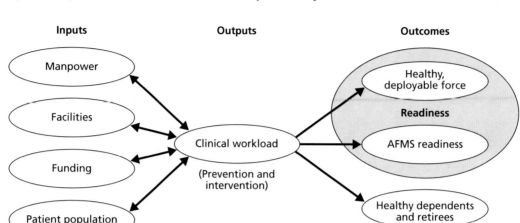

RAND *TR859-1.1*

includes not only the clinical currency of the health-care providers but also predeployment training and availability of supplies and equipment, among other things.[2]

Although this report attempts to describe how AFMS functions in many key areas and related challenges, a particular focus is on the clinical workload the health-care providers handle and its ramifications for the economics of AFMS.

The health care that personnel assigned to an MTF (who can be military, government civilians, or contractors) provide is termed *direct care*; the care the Department of Defense (DoD) purchases from civilian medical providers for the military beneficiary population (active duty, dependents, and retirees)—typically under TRICARE contracts—is termed *purchased care*. The vast majority of the health care active-duty members receive is direct care at MTFs. However, in fiscal year (FY) 2006, about 55 percent of all health care for the military beneficiary population was purchased at civilian institutions under TRICARE, the health benefit program for active-duty military, retirees, and dependents and some reserve component personnel and their dependents (see Bigelow, Harris, and Hillestad, 2008, p. 2, Table 1.1). The percentage of health care purchased from civilian providers has continued to increase since 2006.

One MHS operating principle is to provide as much direct care to beneficiaries as facility and personnel capacity allows, thereby minimizing expenses for purchased care and maximizing clinical currency opportunities. However, readiness demands, which take providers away from their normal clinical settings, can reduce the amount of work an MTF can accomplish on a day-to-day basis. A reduction in the medical personnel at an MTF due to deployments and other military duties creates a need either to find substitute providers to replace deployed personnel in the MTF or to "refer patients downtown," to civilian providers. But because patients will want to maintain continuity with their civilian providers, these referrals can mean that the workloads will continue to be lower and training opportunities fewer even after deployments

---

[2] Throughout this report, clinical currency describes what medical personnel possess who have received the required training and experience to perform their medical duties without further training, instruction, or experience. Thus, a surgeon would be clinically current if he or she were capable of performing surgery in his or her specialty immediately after arriving at a deployment site.

have ended. This is an especially serious problem for hospitals because inpatient care provides the work necessary to maintain currency among the critical-care surgeons, nurses, and technicians who are most needed for wartime surgery.

The Challenge to the Military Health System

MHS faces an ongoing problem similar to that of the rest of the military: how it can train realistically in peacetime and maintain readiness to perform its duties effectively in wartime. There are two unique aspects of the MHS readiness problem.

First, the initial screening process for acceptance into the military services produces a young, healthy group of individuals, generally with few chronic medical problems. As a result, the active-duty population offers few peacetime opportunities for the medical services to practice the critical-care skills required in wartime. Dependents and retirees, on the other hand, especially the older retiree population, generally offer more-complicated health-care cases, providing significant training opportunities.

Second, the patient demographics change significantly during wartime. Although much of the work necessary to care for a deployed military population requires addressing the same routine injuries and illnesses as in peacetime, combat can dramatically increase the number and severity of injuries and wounds. Severe trauma cases occur regularly in high-intensity combat environments, such as those in Iraq and Afghanistan (especially among Army and Marine Corps personnel). Yet these types of wounds and injuries are seldom seen in the non-deployed (i.e., "peacetime") environment in the DoD beneficiary group. Thus, it is difficult for the military medical departments to train critical-care specialists—those who are needed to treat trauma cases—in peacetime. As a secondary effect, it is difficult to recruit and retain critical-care specialists if they have only limited opportunities to practice their skills during peacetime (see Keating et al., 2009).

In addition to the difficulty of training military medical personnel for wartime, lower peacetime workloads inevitably lead to a focus on efficiency. The administration, Congress, and the American people have been very supportive of efforts to ensure that military personnel receive high-quality medical care (especially during the global war on terror [GWOT]). However, DoD and other agencies have forecast continued increases in DoD health-care costs, which have attracted the attention of those who want some measure of efficiency along with effectiveness. For example, in 2003, the Congressional Budget Office (CBO) noted that MHS costs had doubled in real terms since 1988 and predicted that they would continue to grow from $27 billion in 2003 to between $40 billion and $52 billion (in constant dollars) in 2020 if military health care followed U.S. per capita trends.

According to DoD data, an aging population, rising medical fees, and congressionally mandated enhancements to the TRICARE benefit more than doubled the annual cost of military health care from $19 billion in 2001 to $38 billion in 2006; the cost was nearly $40 billion in FY 2007 (Defense Health Program [DHP], undated, p. 4). Assuming no further changes to the TRICARE benefit, costs are projected to climb to $64 billion by 2015, consuming roughly 11.3 percent of the defense budget, up from 8 percent in FY 2006 (Colarusso and

Bender, 2007). Attention has focused particularly on the Navy and Air Force medical activities, because their direct-care workload has dropped significantly since FY 2000.[3]

Furthermore, the FY 2005 Base Realignment and Closure (BRAC) Commission recommended a major reduction in DoD inpatient capacity, to be achieved in part by converting five AFMS hospitals to ambulatory (outpatient) surgical centers (ASCs) and merging two stand-alone clinics with U.S. Army medical organizations.[4]

Purpose

With AFMS facing these challenges, the Deputy Surgeon General of the Air Force asked RAND Project AIR FORCE to evaluate its current situation, with particular emphasis on

- evaluating how AFMS functions as a health plan, a health-care provider, and a payer for services, as well as how it relates to other DoD organizations
- examining how resource decisions are made and how the Medical Expense and Performance Reporting System (MEPRS) and other systems and processes affect resource allocation within MHS
- analyzing the effects of resource decisions on system incentives and medical readiness
- examining alternative methodologies for solving problems that are discovered.

Methodology

RAND project staff interviewed a wide range of officials in OASD(HA), the TRICARE Management Activity (TMA), Air Force and other military services' headquarters medical staffs, U.S. Air Force and Army MTFs, and the Veterans Health Administration (VHA). Our analysis is based on information obtained from these interviews and data from the Air Force, OASD(HA), and published health-care sources. These interviews and the data analysis allowed us to better understand the current situation in AFMS and to provide potential options for improvement.

Organization of This Report

Chapter Two examines the AFMS mission; its history from the 1990s to the present; relationships among AFMS and OASD(HA), TMA, the other services' medical departments, and U.S. Air Force major commands (MAJCOMs); and key differences among the service medical organizations.

---

[3]   In an opening statement to a hearing of the Military Personnel Subcommittee of the House Armed Services Committee, chairwoman Susan Davis (D-Calif.) noted that DoD health-care expenditures were rising rapidly and soon would account for over 11 percent of the total DoD budget. She noted that costs needed to be controlled or else Congress would be facing some difficult questions on what to fund and what promises to keep (Davis, 2008). See Chapter Five for further discussion of the AFMS workload.

[4]   The hospitals are located at Lackland Air Force Base (AFB), Andrews AFB, the Air Force Academy, MacDill AFB, and Scott AFB. The hospital at Keesler AFB was initially recommended for conversion, but was later removed from the list.

Chapter Three discusses AFMS funding, the process used to develop AFMS funding requirements, and sources of funding and differences between them. It also describes OASD(HA) initiatives to adjust funding based on workload and efficiency goals, the effects of these initiatives on AFMS funding, differences between costs and earnings at MTFs, and the current adequacy of AFMS funding.

Chapter Four evaluates one of the major cost and workload accounting systems the services' medical departments use (MEPRS), other systems used to report workloads, the effect on AFMS of underreported workloads, and some planned improvements to MHS reporting systems.

Chapter Five describes changes in the services' medical system workloads since FY 2000 and analyzes the reasons for the decline in AFMS workloads. It also estimates the amount of workload lost to deployments and other readiness requirements for medical personnel.

Chapter Six outlines four options for recapturing and/or increasing the inpatient workloads of AFMS critical-care specialists.

Chapter Seven provides overall conclusions and addresses the key issues that AFMS faces or will face in the future.

CHAPTER TWO

Overview of the Air Force Medical Service

This chapter describes AFMS's mission and recent history, its relationships with OASD(HA), TMA, the other military services, and the Air Force MAJCOMs. It also discusses the differences among the services' health-care approaches, organizations, and funding.

Mission

The Air Force Surgeon General's web page provides the following vision and mission for AFMS:

> **AFMS Vision:** Provide quality, world-class healthcare and health service support to eligible beneficiaries anywhere in the world at anytime.

> **AFMS Mission:** The AFMS provides seamless health service support to the USAF and combatant commanders. The AFMS assists in sustaining the performance, health and fitness of every Airman. It promotes and advocates for optimizing human performance (sustainment and enhancement) for the warfighters, including the optimal integration of human capabilities with systems. The AFMS operates and manages a worldwide healthcare system capable of responding to a full spectrum of anticipated health requirements and provides an integrated healthcare system from forward deployed locations through definitive care with an emphasis on prevention of illness and injury. It arranges for healthcare capabilities that it does not possess organically. It directly supports USAF operations and theater aeromedical evacuation (AE) of joint and combined forces. (Air Force Surgeon General, undated)

To accomplish its mission, AFMS has about 40,000 officer, enlisted, and civilian personnel in the active force and another 20,000 personnel in the Air National Guard and Air Force Reserve. It is responsible for providing health care to about 2.6 million active-duty personnel, retirees, and dependents. The AFMS annual budget is approximately $5 billion.[1] It operates 74 permanent MTFs in the United States and overseas, in which it conducted more than 38,000 inpatient admissions and about 7 million outpatient visits in FY 2007. Its forces are deployed around the world, including significant numbers of personnel temporarily deployed. For example, in FY 2007, the equivalent of nearly 153 clinicians and 132 nurses were deployed throughout the year. As DoD's lead service for the AE mission, AFMS transports wounded and injured personnel via fixed-wing aircraft with trained and equipped aeromedical crews both within

---

[1] Chapter Three offers more details on the budget.

theaters of operation and from theaters of operation to higher echelons of care, such as from Iraq to Germany or the United States.

Recent History

Since Operation Desert Storm in 1991, two significant changes have had a major effect on AFMS: the reduction and transformation of its MTFs and reorganizations of AFMS forces for deployment during contingencies and wartime, both of which mirrored trends in the rest of the Air Force.

In the years since Operation Desert Storm, the number of AFMS MTFs has decreased from 120 in 1992 to 74 in FY 2007 (see Figure 2.1). This reduction was due primarily to base closures, starting in the early 1990s, as part of the overall reduction in the DoD footprint under the BRAC process. In a few cases, AFMS MTFs were closed when the Air Force's responsibilities for health care in certain areas were merged with those of other services' MTFs. In addition, the number of inpatient facilities (medical centers and hospitals) was drastically reduced from 76 in FY 1992 to just 15 in FY 2008, with further reductions planned for the following five years.

There are three main reasons for transforming some inpatient facilities (hospitals) to stand-alone clinics or ASCs. First, concerned about the quality of care, AFMS elected to convert some hospitals primarily because their inpatient workloads were not great enough to maintain the clinical currency of the assigned physicians, nurses, and technicians assigned.[2] A second

Figure 2.1
Air Force Medical Service Treatment Facilities, FYs 1992–2013

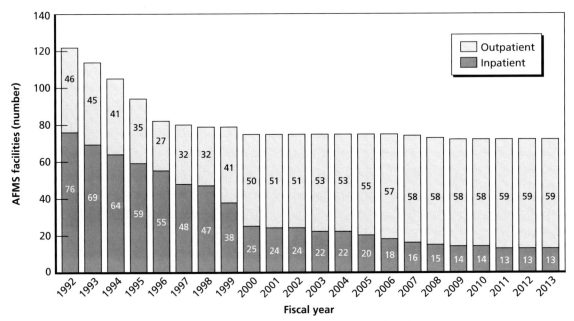

SOURCE: HQ AF/SG8P spreadsheet, "AFMS MTF Hospital Clinic Inventory," undated.
RAND TR859-2.1

---

2   Based on interviews with current and past AFMS personnel.

driver was a national shift in health-care services—especially certain surgical procedures—from inpatient to outpatient (ASC) settings. The third and most recent driver was the FY 2005 BRAC, which, among other decisions, directed the conversion of five Air Force hospitals into clinics with ASCs. The rationale for these conversions (and for those of several Army and Navy hospitals) was that DoD could

> rely on the civilian medical network for inpatient services at these installations. This recommendation supports strategies of reducing excess capacity and locating military personnel in activities with higher military value with a more diverse workload, providing them with enhanced opportunities to maintain their medical currency to meet COCOM [combatant commander] requirements. Additionally, a robust network with available inpatient capacity of Joint Accreditation of Hospital Organizations and/or Medicare accredited civilian/Veterans Affairs hospitals is located within 40 miles of the referenced facilities. (BRAC, 2005)

Many of AFMS's inpatient facilities were quite modest, given the number of inpatient beds at the 76 hospitals open in 1992 (see Figure 2.2). About 60 percent of the inpatient MTFs had 25 or fewer beds. Maintaining small hospitals not only was expensive but also limited the number of specialties that could maintain clinical currency and quality of care, given the limited patient workload.

Over the same period, AFMS gradually began to focus on primary care and maintenance of a healthy force and shifted its doctrinal emphasis from intervention to prevention. It is unclear whether this caused closure of the smaller hospitals or was in reaction to them.

Also during the same period, the Air Force as a whole changed how it would plan for and structure its deployable force. Because of continuous deployment requirements (or a high probability of units being deployed), the Air Force developed the Air Expeditionary Force

Figure 2.2
Comparison of Air Force Medical Service Hospitals in 1992 and 2008, by Size and Number

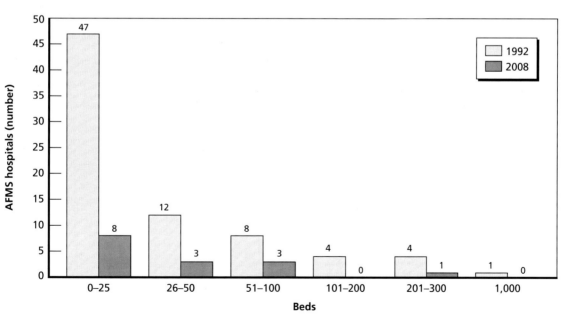

SOURCE: HQ AF/SG8P spreadsheet, "AFMS MTF Hospital Clinic Inventory," undated.
RAND TR859-2.2

(AEF) concept. Deployable units are assigned to one of ten AEFs. Pairs of AEFs must be ready for deployment during specified three-month (later four-month) periods, after which they are replaced by the next AEF pair, and so on. The goal was to forecast when units would be deployed (or available for deployment) to give Air Force personnel more predictability in their lives. To support this concept, AFMS created five medical AEFs, each of which supports one of the five operational AEF pairs. These medical AEFs are flexible but are fashioned to support the Air Force population in the AEFs (the "Air Force population at risk"). This doctrine was similar to that of the Army and Navy, which likewise designed their medical forces to support their own populations at risk.

The Air Force's AE force was designed to support evacuation of the injured and wounded of the services during operational deployments. Thus, AFMS deployment doctrine shifted from its 1990s posture of deploying large air-transportable hospitals designed to treat and hold large numbers of patients in combat theaters to supporting the Air Force population at risk, focusing on stabilizing then rapidly evacuating wounded or seriously ill personnel from the theater.[3]

This concept remained in effect until AFMS was tasked to support three in-theater hospitals in Iraq, Afghanistan, and Qatar as part of GWOT. AFMS initially staffed the hospital at Qatar, then assumed responsibility for the theater hospital at Balad Air Base (AB), Iraq, in 2004, and took the lead at the Craig Joint Theater Hospital at Bagram AB, Afghanistan, in 2006.

These taskings required a different mix of medical personnel from those of the medical AEFs, with an increased requirement for critical-care personnel (surgeons, operating room personnel, etc.) because the injured and wounded of all services were being treated at these hospitals. AFMS has been able to meet these new in-theater hospital requirements, although some specialties have been tasked well in excess of the utilization rates anticipated in AFMS requirements determination and planning.

In particular, the utilization of critical-care and mental health specialists has been higher than expected. Supporting these in-theater requirements means that fewer of these personnel are available to provide health care at their home MTFs. Chapter Five will discuss this challenge in more detail.

Overview of the DoD Military Health System

The entire DoD MHS serves more than 9 million eligible active-duty personnel, retirees, and their dependents. Health care for this population is provided either at MTFs or through purchased care. DoD purchases the latter primarily from civilian providers, although some care comes from other federal providers, most notably the U.S. Department of Veterans Affairs (VA).

MHS policy guidance is under the purview of the Under Secretary of Defense for Personnel and Readiness and is promulgated by OASD(HA). TMA (a field activity that operates under the authority, direction, and control of OASD(HA) and the three military departments' medical services fund and manage health-care delivery. The overall responsibilities of OASD(HA) are found in DoD Directive (DoDD) 5136.01 (pp. 2–3):

---

[3] For a full discussion of the AFMS expeditionary medical support (EMEDS) concept, see Snyder et al., 2009.

The Assistant Secretary of Defense for Health Affairs (ASD[HA]) is the principal advisor to the Secretary of Defense and the USD(P&R) for all DoD health policies, programs, and force health protection activities. The ASD(HA) shall ensure the effective execution of the Department's medical mission, providing and maintaining readiness for medical services and support to: members of the Armed Forces including during military operations; their dependents; those held in the control of the Armed Forces; and others entitled to or eligible for DoD medical care and benefits, including under the TRICARE Program. In carrying out these responsibilities, the ASD(HA) shall exercise authority, direction, and control over the DoD medical and dental personnel authorizations and policy, facilities, programs, funding, and other resources in the Department of Defense.

The bullets describe some of ASD(HA)'s key responsibilities the directive outlines that relate to the economics and readiness of MHS (DoDD 5136.01, pp. 3–4):

- Review and evaluate DoD health and medical programs.
- Undertake management oversight activities as required to ensure health and medical policies, plans, programs, systems, and standards are compatible and support the Total Force objectives and requirements and enhance readiness.
- Serve as program manager for all DoD health and medical resources.
- Prepare and submit, in the DoD planning, programming, budgeting, and execution (PPBE) process, a DoD Unified Medical Program budget to provide resources for the DoD MHS.
- Present and justify the DoD Unified Medical Program budget throughout the PPBE process, including representations before the Congress.
- Obtain submissions of the medical program needs of the commanders of the Combatant Commands, through the Chairman of the Joint Chiefs of Staff. Obtain submissions from the Secretaries of the military departments of their proposed elements of the DoD Unified Medical Program and budget, and integrate those submissions, as appropriate.
- Serve as the principal advisor to the USD(P&R) and the Secretary of Defense on deployment matters as they pertain to force health in DoD, including aspects of policy, readiness, and medical research.
- Develop plans, policies, and programs to facilitate new or improved force health protection initiatives and support the investigation, information exchange, reporting, and archiving of pertinent health related information on past, present, or potential military deployments.

However, ASD(HA) does not have line authority over the service medical departments and must communicate with the heads of DoD components, as necessary, to carry out assigned responsibilities and functions, including the transmission of requests for advice and assistance. Communications to the military departments must be transmitted through the secretaries of the military departments, their designees, or as otherwise provided in law or directed by the Secretary of Defense in other DoD issuances. Communications to the commanders of the combatant commands is normally transmitted through the Chairman of the Joint Chiefs of Staff. (DoDD 5136.01, p. 6)

ASD(HA) may also not direct a change in the structure of the chain of command within a military department or with respect to medical personnel assigned to that command.

TMA's major responsibilities include

- executing the TRICARE program—serving as the program manager for TRICARE health and medical resources, supervising and administering TRICARE programs, funding, and other resources[4]
- issuing, through the service secretaries, program direction for the policy execution within MHS to the surgeons general of the Army, Navy, and Air Force
- supporting ASD(HA)'s presentation and justification of the DoD Unified Medical Program and budget throughout the PPBE process, including representations before Congress
- managing and executing DHP and DoD Unified Medical Program accounts,[5] including military department execution of allocated funds, in accordance with ASD(HA) instructions, fiscal guidance from the Under Secretary of Defense (Comptroller), and applicable law.[6]

Altogether, the Unified Medical Program amounted to $39.9 billion in FY 2007 (including supplemental funding of $1.9 billion). ASD(HA) controls all this funding (via TMA) throughout the DoD PPBE System phases. Because Congress appropriates the MILPERS and MILCON funds for the services, ASD(HA) exerts control during the first three phases of the PPBE (specifically, planning, programming, and budgeting), but the services manage execution of these two appropriations. Thus, during the preparation of the program objective memorandum (POM), budget estimate submission, and President's Budget, ASD(HA) controls the allocation and justification of much of the MILPERS and MILCON funds related to MHS. However, once these funds have been appropriated, the services have the authority to execute the MILPERS and MILCON appropriations directly.

Key Differences Among the Services' Health Systems

The medical services have many differences, but we will focus on the following three key differences in the way the services structure and command their medical forces:

- their size and composition
- their command structures
- the number and size of their medical facilities.

Size and Composition

The personnel authorizations in all three medical services are a combination of DHP and the service ("line") authorizations. As shown in Table 2.1, the FY 2008 projected end-strength of each service differs significantly in terms of overall numbers, military-civilian mix, and authorizations.

---

[4] ASD(HA) also serves as Director, TMA.

[5] The Unified Medical Program refers to the total funding for MHS. DHP funds consist of the operation and maintenance (O&M), procurement, and research and development (R&D) amounts appropriated to DoD and allocated to the service medical organizations during budget execution; the Unified Medical Program includes the DHP appropriations plus the military personnel (MILPERS) and military construction (MILCON) funds related to the medical function that are appropriated directly to the services. See Chapter Three for more information on the funding process.

[6] DoDD 5136.01, paragraph 6.2.

Ninety-three percent of AFMS medical personnel are on DHP authorizations; the rest are part of the line (Air Force). Two major functions that are part of the line are AE forces and the squadron medical element personnel (primarily flight surgeons). In addition, approximately 80 percent of AFMS personnel are in uniform. With minor exceptions, all medical personnel on an Air Force base are normally assigned to the base MTF.

In contrast, the Army medical force is about double the size of AFMS, and nearly 50 percent of the uniformed medical personnel are in the line. A large part of the Army medical force (mainly enlisted medics) is assigned to operational units, not MTFs, on a day-to-day basis. In fact, as Table 2.1 shows, the line has 31 percent of all Army medical personnel (military and civilians). The Army also has a much higher percentage of civilian medical personnel (38 percent).

The Navy falls in between the other two services in most statistics; 20 percent of its medical personnel are in the line, and it has a slightly higher percentage of civilian personnel than does AFMS. Two major groups of the medical personnel in the Navy line are those assigned to ships (both officers and enlisted) and medics assigned to Marine Corps operational units, because the Navy Medical Service is responsible for both Navy and Marine Corps health care.

These differences among the services have evolved over time.[7] Although DHP appropriations were established in 1992, the consequences of the services' early decisions about medical funding persist today. AFMS must justify nearly all its funding with OASD(HA) and TMA during the POM and budget processes, while the Army and Navy have a more balanced mix of line and DHP authorizations. Each service's financing method is unique, much like their

Table 2.1
Projected FY 2008 Active-Duty Medical End Strengths

| | | Military | | Civilian | | Total | | |
		End Strength	Service Percentage	FTEs	Service Percentage	Personnel	Service Percentage	Civilian Percentage
Army	DHP	26,241	54	27,478	92	53,719	69	51.2
	Line	22,000	46	2,500	8	24,500	31	10.2
	Total	48,241		29,978	100	78,219		38.3
Navy	DHP	29,465	75	11,015	100	40,480	80	27.2
	Line	10,000	25	0	0	10,000	20	0.0
	Total	39,465	100	11,015	100	50,480		21.8
Air Force	DHP	31,365	94	7,310	91	38,675	93	18.9
	Line	2,133	6	730	9	2,863	7	25.5
	Total	33,498	100	8,040	100	41,538		19.4
Total	DHP	87,071	72	45,803	93	132,874	78	32.8
	Line	34,133	28	3,230	7	37,363	22	8.6
	Total	121,204	100	49,033	100	170,237		27.5

SOURCE: FY 2008 TRICARE Management Activity POM submission.

---

[7] These divisions between line and DHP positions and dollars were initially established in Program Budget Decision 742, 1991, which consolidated all medical resources under ASD(HA). Military personnel funds and resources in support of field or numbered medical units, hospital ships, and shipboard medical operations were exempt from this consolidation. This policy became effective in the FY 1992 DoD budget.

organization, locations, and support to the operational forces. In our interviews, we found that no single approach had clear advantages or disadvantages over the others, and all are designed to meet their parent services' medical needs.

Command Structure

A second key difference is the services' command structure for the medical forces. Both the Army and the Navy have a medical command—the U.S. Army Medical Command and the U.S. Navy Bureau of Medicine and Surgery, respectively—that directly commands its medical forces in MTFs. Thus, an Army or Navy MTF commander on an installation may report to a medical officer who is geographically separated. However, when medical forces are deployed overseas, the medical commander reports to the local operational commander, who is not part of the service's medical command. Thus, in a deployment, a new command relationship is formed between the operational and medical forces.

In contrast, the Air Force medical forces report to the local operational commander at all levels. For example, an Air Force MTF commander reports to the local operational wing commander. In deployed situations, Air Force medical forces will report to the deployed operational commander (i.e., an expeditionary medical group commander will report to the expeditionary wing commander).

In addition, the Air Force Surgeon General is a member of the Headquarters Air Staff but has no day-to-day command relationship with AFMS organizations in the field. In contrast, the surgeons general of the Army and Navy are dual-hatted and have actual command of the medical forces not assigned to operational units on a daily basis. In his or her staff function role, the Air Force Surgeon General advises the Secretary of the Air Force and the Chief of Staff of the Air Force on medical matters, including justifying budgets in the PPBE process, distributing funding, policy guidance, recruiting and training, and assignments, just like the other two surgeons general.

However, compared to the other services, AFMS has a disadvantage in maintaining continuity of care when medical personnel deploy. In AFMS, unlike the Army and Navy, virtually all officer and enlisted medical personnel are assigned to MTFs rather than to operational wings or AEF components. In the Army and Navy, many deploying medical units are organic to maneuver support units, and most of their enlisted personnel are assigned directly to the unit. Some enlisted and most officer medical personnel are part of the Professional Filler system and are pulled from MTFs under a specific support plan. However, since virtually all Air Force medical personnel must be sourced from an MTF, an AFMS deployment is much more likely to disrupt patient care delivery. Much like a manufacturing production line, removing a physician or nurse from an MTF affects provision of health care for the duration of the deployment, unless a backfill can be found. Indeed, MTF production is also lost during predeployment training and during recovery time after medical personnel return. Chapter Five discusses the effects of lost workload on AFMS more fully.

Relationships Between the Air Force Medical Service and Air Force Major Commands

Much like the Air Force Surgeon General, the command surgeons at each of the seven Air Force MAJCOMs also occupy staff positions advising the respective MAJCOM commanders, but they have no command authority over MTFs within their MAJCOMs. As staff members, they are responsible for policy guidance, resourcing, training, assignments, and other noncommand responsibilities.

One difference between AFMS and the other services is that MAJCOM surgeons general have responsibility for funding justification and distribution. Their staffs play a major role working with the Headquarters Air Force Surgeon General staff to prepare the POM and justify medical funding requirements to TMA. During budget execution, the Air Force Surgeon General staff distributes funds to the staffs of the MAJCOM surgeons general, which in turn can use their own discretion to redistribute funding among their MTFs. However, to streamline this process, AFMS has established the Air Force Medical Operating Agency South in San Antonio. This organization consolidated many of the authorizations and duties that were held by the MAJCOMs so that a more centralized and perhaps more consistent set of policies could be applied across a range of AFMS issues.

Medical Facilities

The third difference among the services is in the number and size of the MTFs they operate. As shown previously in Figure 2.1, AFMS operated 74 MTFs in the continental United States (CONUS) and overseas in FY 2007. Table 2.2 shows the number of MTFs operated by each medical service in FY 2007.

AFMS operates fewer inpatient facilities than either the Army or Navy. Unlike the Army and Navy, which use a hub-and-spoke concept under which many small health-care and dental clinics report to geographically separated larger medical organizations, AFMS has a policy of having organizationally independent clinics responsible to the local operational commander. AFMS has argued that each Air Force base requires at least a stand-alone clinic to provide health care not only to the active-duty personnel but also to their dependents, especially where local purchased care may not be readily available. For example, a small hospital at Mountain Home AFB, Idaho, is maintained in a relatively remote area because of the lack of Joint Commission on Accreditation of Healthcare Organizations–approved facilities in that area.

Summary

Each military department medical service has a unique approach to its organization, funding, and facilities that has evolved to meet the operational needs, command philosophy, and deployment concept of its parent service. It is beyond the scope of this project to evaluate the relative effectiveness and efficiency of each service's approach, particularly given the unique wartime and peacetime requirements each must meet. Each has its advantages and disadvan-

Table 2.2
MTFs Operated by Each Medical Service, FY 2007

Service	Medical Centers and Hospitals			Stand-Alone Clinics		
	CONUS[a]	Overseas	Total	CONUS[a]	Overseas	Total
Army	24	4	28	133	37	170
Air Force	10	6	16	52	6	58
Navy[b]	15	7	22	123	28	151

NOTE: Excludes overseas GWOT facilities.
[a] Also includes Alaska and Hawaii.
[b] Includes Marine Corps.

tages, but all were designed to meet the medical needs of their populations. However, some of these differences affect the budgeting process for MTFs (and consequently their earnings), which the next chapter will address.

CHAPTER THREE

Air Force Medical Service Funding

As noted in Chapter One, adequate funding is one of the key ingredients AFMS needs to meet its readiness requirements. This chapter discusses the AFMS funding process, how funding is justified, and the earnings and efficiency measures that can affect funding. We analyze the financial performance of the AFMS MTFs in detail, comparing it with those of the Army and Navy, and examine it in the context of long-term prospects for MHS funding.

Budget Overview

AFMS's total budget in FY 2007 was about $5.2 billion (including GWOT Supplemental funding) and consisted of five appropriations: O&M, procurement, R&D, MILPERS, and MILCON. Generally, Congress funds the overall Air Force through 16 appropriations, which the Air Force manages. However, AFMS receives a mix of Air Force and DHP appropriations. MILPERS and MILCON funds are Air Force appropriations, while O&M, procurement, and R&D are DHP appropriations. The Army and Navy medical program budgets are funded similarly.

ASD(HA) controls only part of AFMS's total funding. During the budget execution year, TMA retains some of the DHP-appropriated funds to pay for purchased care. The rest of the funds are distributed to each of the services to pay for direct care and other medical activities. Table 3.1 shows DHP and service appropriations and each service's total medical funding. The 2007 Unified Medical Program is 72 percent O&M, 25 percent MILPERS, and 3 percent procurement, R&D, and MILCON.

As part of the POM and budget estimate submission phases of DoD's PPBE process, which leads up to the annual President's Budget submission to Congress, OASD(HA) develops the services' medical fiscal guidance controls for the programming portion using a mix of workload-based and historically based allocation methods.[1] Workload-based allocation methods consist of the Prospective Payment System (PPS) and the Medicare Eligible Retiree Health Care Fund (MERHCF). Both these methods, which are described later in this chapter and in detail in Appendixes C and D, are based on workloads forecast for the MTFs. The greater the workload forecast, the more funding is allocated to each service.

---

[1] Fiscal guidance controls are the annual spending limits that the services use to develop their programs during the POM process. Adjustments are made during subsequent OSD-led reviews, so the final funding request in the President's Budget may vary from the initial fiscal guidance. The initial guidance addresses all six years under consideration during the Future Years Defense Program. Thus, during the FY 2010 POM preparation conducted during the first half of 2008, the services programmed FYs 2010–2015.

Table 3.1
MHS Funding in FY 2007

	Appropriation ($M)[a]				
	USA	USN	USAF	TMA	Total
DHP					
O&M	4,080	2,545	2,015	11,609	20,249
Procurement	74	53	66	203	396
R&D	5	30	19	77	131
Total DHP	4,158	2,628	2,100	11,889	20,775
Non-DHP					
MILPERS	2,019	2,381	2,619	0	7,019
MILCON	152	44	87	85	368
Total non-DHP	2,171	2,425	2,706	85	7,387
Unified Medical Program	6,330	5,053	4,806[b]	11,974	28,163

NOTES: Because of rounding, totals may not sum precisely.
The numbers do not include GWOT Supplemental. They also do not include line funding for medical personnel assigned full time to operational units, such as Army medics, Navy medics assigned to Marine Corps units, ship-board medical personnel, Air Force aeromedical personnel, and Air Force personnel assigned to squadron medical elements.

[a] Amounts are in then-year dollars.

[b] In addition to this amount, AFMS received $298.5 million in GWOT supplemental and other funding increases, and collected $117 million in local reimbursements. The Army and Navy also received supplemental and other funding (amounts unavailable). (See the section on local MTF reimbursements.)

The remainder of the POM funding allocation is based on a traditional system, starting with a baseline funding level from a reference year (such as the current appropriation or the President's Budget) and adjusting for known programmatic changes, such as the closure of an MTF or a change in benefits.[2]

In FY 2007, the overall AFMS budget of $5.2 billion (including GWOT supplemental and other funding) was split among the cost of operating the CONUS MTFs,[3] overseas MTFs, and non-MTF operating costs, such as the cost of prescription ingredients, headquarters staff costs, etc. (see Figure 3.1).

Running CONUS MTFs costs about 72 percent of the total AFMS unified budget, or more than $3.76 billion; overseas MTFs spend about 8 percent of the total, or $411 million. Expenses that cannot be tied directly to MTF operations amount to 20 percent, or $1.05 billion.

Figure 3.2 breaks out the total CONUS MTF earnings of $1.6 billion into PPS, MERHCF, and local reimbursements.[4] In budget planning, amounts for two of the three components of earnings, PPS ($906 million) and MERHCF ($577 million), are determined

---

[2]   Fiscal guidance control numbers in recent years have not included GWOT and certain other programs funded by supplemental appropriations.

[3]   Technically, CONUS MTFs would encompass only those in the 48 contiguous states; however, in all calculations, we also included Hawaii and Alaska.

[4]   We define earnings as the portions of the budget that are justified by workload; the rest of the budget is justified by other means, as described previously.

Figure 3.1
Total Air Force Medical Service Obligations, FY 2007

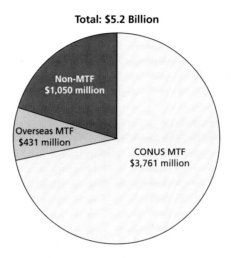

Total: $5.2 Billion

NOTE: To generate this figure, we first sorted the 2007 budget obligations by site into CONUS MTFs (including Alaska and Hawaii), overseas MTFs, and non-MTFs. Next, we subtracted the costs of prescription ingredients from all MTFs, calculated PPS and MERHCF earnings by MTF, then accounted for all MERHCF reimbursements for prescription ingredients. Finally, we added local reimbursements, which appear as negative values in obligations data, into both expenses and earnings.
RAND *TR859-3.1*

Figure 3.2
Total Air Force Medical Service Earnings, FY 2007

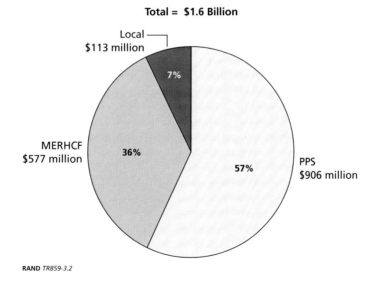

Total = $1.6 Billion

RAND *TR859-3.2*

prospectively (by projecting workloads from previous years). Budget planning does not include local earnings because these consist of reimbursements that are collected through such other means as private insurance. After a patient is seen, individual MTFs file claims with insurance companies and other payers, and are reimbursed directly. Figure 3.2 shows CONUS MTFs only; just $7 million was earned at overseas MTFs, and non-MTFs cannot, by definition, obtain earnings by performing workload.[5]

The $1.6 billion in total AFMS earnings constitutes 31 percent of the total $5.2 billion unified budget. That is, about $3 out of every $10 in the unified budget depends on MTF work and prescriptions; the other $7 is justified by other means in the POM and President's Budget. Separating out the data for CONUS shows that AFMS MTF earnings from PPS, MERHCF, and local sources cover about 42 percent ($1.60 billion/3.76 billion) of operating costs.[6]

Much of the difference between MTF earnings and expenses can be attributed to the inherent costs of running medical facilities that must also meet military requirements: military-unique training of medical personnel, deployments of military medical personnel, and the inefficiencies of operating MTFs in geographical areas with smaller-than-optimal enrolled populations.

Emphasis on Military Treatment Facility Efficiency

With the cost of military health care projected to continue increasing for the foreseeable future and with MHS facing significant shortfalls in funding throughout the FY 2005 POM, ASD(HA) instituted two initiatives designed to increase MTF efficiency by linking a portion of funding to the work performed. The first such initiative was PPS, which was introduced in FY 2005. The second initiative was called the "efficiency wedge." It was initially studied in FY 2005 and partially implemented beginning in FY 2009. However, Congress has disallowed use of the efficiency wedge beginning in FY 2010. These initiatives are examined in greater detail in the following sections.

Prospective Payment System

PPS enables the services to increase their budgets by increasing productivity from a forecast baseline of workload: Part of their funding is based on their workload, rather than their costs.[7] PPS was designed to yield two advantages: First, it would create an incentive for MTFs to deliver more patient care in their existing facilities. Spreading fixed manpower costs and facility expenses over a larger workload would make the MTFs more efficient. Second, increasing the patient workload at MTFs would decrease the need to purchase patient care from civilian health-care providers, thereby reducing the purchased care bill to TMA.

PPS funding levels are determined by the workload at each MTF relative to its baseline workload. The initial baseline was set as the inpatient and outpatient procedures each CONUS

---

[5] PPS is not applied to overseas MTF workload, but MERHCF reimburses for overseas workload performed on TRI-CARE for Life (TFL) enrollees. DoD policy is that PPS should not be applied to overseas locations because they are established according to capabilities assessments as opposed to performance standards. Frequently, overseas MTFs are staffed at high levels to meet capability requirements but do not have as many opportunities to increase workloads as CONUS locations do because of the limited beneficiary populations overseas.

[6] These numbers are shown to provide context for the amounts of expenses and earnings tied to workload completion. Because not all MTF activities result in earnings (readiness activities, other ancillary services under PPS, etc.), even the most efficient MTF could not earn 100 percent of its expenses. The Office of the Secretary of Defense (OSD) has studies under way to expand workload definitions and associated earnings, so these percentages should increase over time as new workloads are quantified.

[7] See Appendix C for additional information on PPS.

MTF performed in FY 2003.[8] Then, beginning in FY 2005, workloads were forecast for future years; divergences from the baseline were priced using a local, procedure-specific, Civilian Health and Medical Program of the Uniformed Services (CHAMPUS) Maximum Allowable Charge, a Medicare-like reimbursement rate for each MTF. If the forecast or actual workload in subsequent years was less than in the baseline year, funding would be reduced; if greater, funding would be increased. However, the PPS methodology did not account for prescriptions and other ancillary services. Because the funding adjustments (increases or reductions) occurred during the budget execution year, they could apply only to DHP O&M funding allocations through FY 2007; MILPERS funding could not be adjusted during the year of execution. However, beginning with the FY 2008 POM, both the MILPERS and O&M appropriations were adjusted during the POM and budget deliberations. In addition, the O&M appropriation continued to be adjusted during the execution year, and the actual workload accomplished by the midyear time frame was compared to the projections for each year.

During PPS implementation, OASD(HA) gradually phased in the adjustments: 25 percent of the full calculated amount in FY 2005, 50 percent in FY 2006, 75 percent in FY 2007, and the full adjustment in FY 2008. PPS reduced Navy and Air Force funding but modestly increased Army funding because its workload increased over the FY 2003 baseline.[9]

For FY 2008, the baseline was changed from the FY 2003 to the FY 2007 workload. The net effect of this workload baseline update was an execution year reduction of $28 million to AFMS O&M in FY 2008, a little less than 2 percent of the AFMS budget. However, making this cut during the execution year meant AFMS had less flexibility to manage it across appropriations than it would have had with a reduction in the POM, which can be spread over any combination of appropriations, including the MILPERS account. By the FY 2010 POM, the full PPS adjustment reduced the AFMS budget by a total of about $63 million. However, with other adjustments from the POM baseline development, including an AFMS commitment to increase its workload by $46 million in FY 2010, the net effect was an increase of $16 million to the FY 2010 baseline funding. During the FY 2010 execution year, further adjustments will be made based on the actual workload, but only to the O&M account. Thus, AFMS's funding could decrease if it does not meet its commitment to increase its workload.

Although OASD(HA) calculates these adjustments for each MTF, the services can spread adjustments across their respective medical organizations as they see fit. AFMS did not penalize individual MTFs for their decreased earnings; the staff at Headquarters Air Force allocated reductions during the POM or budget distribution processes. This policy has the effect of shifting PPS incentive to increase workload away from the managers of individual MTFs, which carry the workload, to the managers of the entire AFMS. AFMS's approach was somewhat different than those of the Army and Navy, which tended to implement reductions at the MTF level.

Efficiency Wedge

The "efficiency wedge" was an outgrowth of two studies conducted in 2004 and 2005: the TMA "Valuation Study" and the "Red/Yellow/Green" study.[10] In the Valuation Study, which

---

[8]   In this report, CONUS includes MTFs in Alaska and Hawaii.

[9]   See Chapter Five for details on workload trends in all three services.

[10]   Our interviewees cited these studies specifically. See Appendix E for more information on the efficiency wedge.

was based on FY 2003 data, OSD found that the cost of care that all CONUS MTFs provided exceeded the cost of purchasing equivalent care from the private sector by $3.7 billion, or 56 percent. The study also found that MTF pharmacies had a cost advantage over civilian pharmacies because they used the federal ceiling price structure for drug purchases.[11]

The Red/Yellow/Green study examined differences in the cost of care among groups of MTFs with similar characteristics. Study members assigned all 360 DoD MTFs to 14 peer groups based on such factors as size, type of care (inpatient or ambulatory only), and location (CONUS or overseas). The study found a wide variation in the cost of care within peer groups. It estimated that having the most costly MTFs in each group reduce their costs to within 25 percent of the mean cost per workload unit for their peer group could yield significant savings. However, it did not recommend changes for MTFs that had lower-than-average costs for their peer group. MTFs with costs in the upper 25th percentile of their peer group were targeted for efficiency-wedge reductions. The total AFMS efficiency-wedge bill was $647.4 million, taken incrementally across FY 2006 to FY 2009. Later, TMA updated the study and reduced the services and savings forecasts. Ultimately, the reductions in FYs 2006–2008 were cut to $192 million and the $323 million FY 2009 reduction was decreased to $114 million. Congress precluded any more efficiency-wedge reductions in FY 2010 and beyond.[12]

It would be difficult to measure the true effects of the efficiency-wedge budget reductions because all the services' budgets increased significantly more than the President's Budget during these years, mostly through supplemental funding. In the case of AFMS, Congress added almost $1 billion in FYs 2006 through 2008 to the President's Budget request.

Medicare-Eligible Retiree Health Care Fund Earnings

MERHCF was established after passage of the TFL legislation in the FY 2001 National Defense Authorization Act.[13] TFL's provisions apply to Medicare-eligible military retirees, dependents, and survivors—about 2 million health-care beneficiaries across DoD. The TFL program pays for health care and prescriptions for this dual-eligible (Medicare and TFL) population by purchasing care from civilian sources. Under TFL, DoD is the second payer to Medicare, covering about 20 percent of the allowable cost for purchased care, thereby eliminating any need for the beneficiaries to pay for health care. However, MERHCF was established to encourage MTFs to continue providing health care to these beneficiaries on a space-available basis by providing the MTFs earnings for this care.

In FY 2007, MERHCF earnings totaled $580.9 million, more than one-half of all AFMS earnings. Within this total, inpatient earnings AFMS-wide amounted to $124 million; ambulatory earnings were $139 million; and pharmacy prescription earnings were $318 million. However, pharmacy earnings include the cost of the drugs dispensed ($249 million), which

---

[11] The Veterans Health Care Act of 1992 mandated that drug manufacturers offer discounts to federal agencies. TMA estimates that MTF pharmacies save about 24 percent compared to retail prices for the same drugs.

[12] The Senate Appropriations Committee language on the FY 2008 DoD Appropriations Bill (Senate Report 110-155) stated that the "Committee strongly encourages the Department to review its FY 2009 budget and future year program and remove the efficiency wedge. Given the current wartime environment, the Department cannot afford to take such risk in our MHS. For as long as there are ongoing war efforts, our MTFs will need all the resources available."

[13] See Appendix D for more information on MERHCF.

can be considered "pass-through" costs. Thus, only the net earnings of $69 million can be considered an offset to MTF operating costs.

MERHCF has both similarities to and differences from PPS. Unlike PPS, both CONUS and overseas MTFs receive purchased care payments.[14] But like PPS, purchased care is prospective: A forecast based on a previous fiscal year serves as a baseline for calculating the next fiscal year's earnings. For example, the FY 2006 workload was used as the baseline for FY 2008.[15] Measurements of the quantity and type of care each MTF provides are based on the inpatient, ambulatory, and prescription workloads. The actual cost of providing the care at each MTF (including MILPERS costs), as collected in MEPRS, is used to calculate and forecast earnings, instead of the CHAMPUS Maximum Allowable Charge (CMAC) rate PPS uses. Because the cost of care at MTFs is generally higher than this rate, MERHCF often provides a higher reimbursement than PPS does for the same services offered at the same MTF. An interesting note is that PPS also pays for the same inpatient and ambulatory health-care procedures provided to the same beneficiaries as MERHCF. In some sense, a CONUS MTF is paid twice for the same procedure.

Local Military Treatment Facility Reimbursements

MTFs are allowed to collect reimbursements from third-party payers for health care provided to beneficiaries who have other health insurance (for instance, a spouse of an active-duty member who has employer-sponsored health insurance) or to nonbeneficiaries who receive emergency care. In these cases, the insurer would be billed for services rendered in an MTF.[16] Under this program, the MTF can use the funds it collects in excess of its collection costs for local operating purposes. These funds are considered part of the MTF's Total Obligational Authority (DoDI 6015.23, 2002). In FY 2007, AFMS collected a total of $117 million from third parties.

Military Treatment Facility Financial Information

To provide better insight into AFMS health-care costs and earnings, as well as those of the Army and Navy for comparison, this section analyzes the costs of operating the different types of CONUS MTFs and the earnings they receive from PPS, MERHCF, and local reimbursements.[17] To do so, we removed several categories of MTF expenses and some revenues. We included only the expenses directly related to patient care: military personnel, civilian and contractor personnel, and O&M for equipment and facilities. We included the earnings and costs of running pharmacies and separately identify the earnings and expenses for prescription ingredients. We removed the costs of headquarters staffs, air expeditionary forces, and other non–care-related administrative expenses.

---

[14] Overseas earnings from MERHCF are about $7 million.

[15] Unlike PPS, which conducts midyear reviews and adjusts funding according to workload accomplishments compared to the baseline, MERHCF does not conduct such reviews at midyear.

[16] Under the authority of 10 USC 1079b and 1095 and Executive Order 9397.

[17] We analyze only CONUS MTFs because overseas MTFs do not receive PPS earnings.

AFMS operates a mix of inpatient hospitals and ambulatory facilities. The operating costs of these two types of facilities have significant differences. Indeed, after making our adjustments, we found that the total cost of operating the 11 CONUS AFMS hospitals exceeded the total cost of operating the 51 CONUS stand-alone clinics in FY 2007 (see Figure 3.3).[18] AFMS spends about 48 cents of each operating dollar on the 11 hospitals, 37 cents on the 51 clinics, and 15 cents are spent on ingredients at hospital and clinic pharmacies.

Even though the hospitals are more expensive to operate, they generate more earnings than the clinics do, as shown in Figure 3.3. Through PPS, MERHCF, and local reimbursements, hospitals earned about 56 percent of their operating costs, while stand-alone clinics earned only 25 percent on average.[19] This difference is due to reimbursement rates for different types of work: An inpatient admission earns on the order of $11,000, while an ambulatory visit might only earn $75 dollars. That said, inpatient procedures are also far more resource intensive (i.e., more costly) than outpatient visits.

Figure 3.4 breaks out the expenses and earnings of AFMS CONUS hospitals individually. The figure does not include costs and reimbursements for prescription ingredients but does include the earnings and costs of dispensing the prescriptions. Individual expenses are shown for military personnel salaries of assigned personnel, base and facility O&M expenses (utilities, painting and repair, etc.), and O&M expenses related to medical care (operating room

Figure 3.3
Expenses and Earnings for Air Force Medical Service Facilities in CONUS (including prescription ingredient costs)

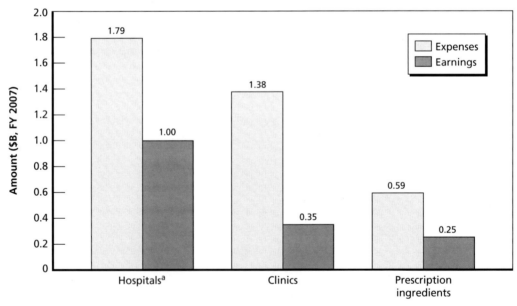

[a]Includes expenses and estimated earnings for Keesler AFB.
RAND *TR859-3.3*

---

[18] The total expenses shown are the same as those in Figure 3.1 for CONUS MTF obligations.

[19] MERHCF reimburses 42 percent of total AFMS prescription ingredients. PPS does not reimburse for prescription ingredients. All local reimbursements were attributed to the hospitals or clinics where they were earned, because the data did not allow us to separate pharmacy costs. However, these costs should be a small part of local reimbursements.

Figure 3.4
Expenses and Earnings for Air Force Medical Service Hospitals in CONUS

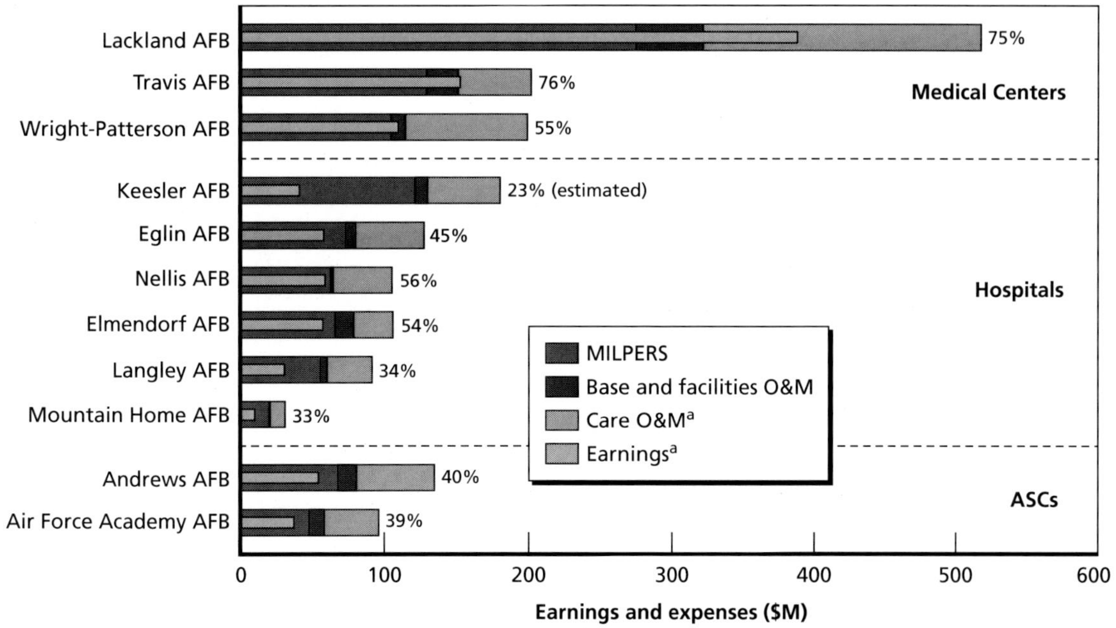

NOTE: Amounts in FY 2007 dollars.
ª *Excluding* prescription ingredients.
RAND *TR859-3.4*

supplies, oxygen, rubber gloves, etc.). Total earnings are shown for PPS, MERHCF, and local reimbursement collections.

Wilford Hall Medical Center (WHMC) at Lackland AFB, Texas, is by far the largest MTF in AFMS (based on both annual expenses and annual earnings). It earns about 75 percent of its operating costs and about 25 percent of total AFMS earnings.[20] In contrast, the earnings at the Keesler AFB hospital are very low because of extensive damage during Hurricane Katrina in FY 2005; the MTF was just returning to full operation of inpatient services in FY 2007. Mountain Home AFB hospital is in a geographically isolated portion of Idaho, with few civilian alternatives for inpatient health care in the immediate area. This MTF provides an example of how difficult it is to recover the costs required to run a small, remote hospital with a comparatively small enrolled population. Two MTFs listed as hospitals (Andrews AFB and the Air Force Academy hospital) have recently been converted to ASCs with no inpatient capabilities.[21]

In contrast to the CONUS hospitals, which averaged earnings of 56 percent of operating costs, the 51 AFMS stand-alone clinics averaged earnings of 25 percent of their costs (see Figure 3.5).

---

[20] See Appendix E for a discussion of these costs and the projected effects of the merger of WHMC and Brooke Army Medical Center (BAMC).

[21] ASCs are a rapidly growing trend in U.S. health care. In 1980, there were 275 ASCs; in 2006, there were almost 5,200. Most ASCs are specialty, "boutique" clinics that offer certain scheduled procedures, such as eye surgery and orthopedics, and do not require hospitalization.

Comparing the Air Force Medical Service to the Army and Navy Medical Departments

Given the propensity to compare military medical departments' health-care services along the lines of peacetime metrics—cost, revenue, productivity, and efficiency, for instance—a logical

Figure 3.5
PPS, MERHCF, and Local Earnings for Air Force Medical Service Stand-Alone Clinics in CONUS

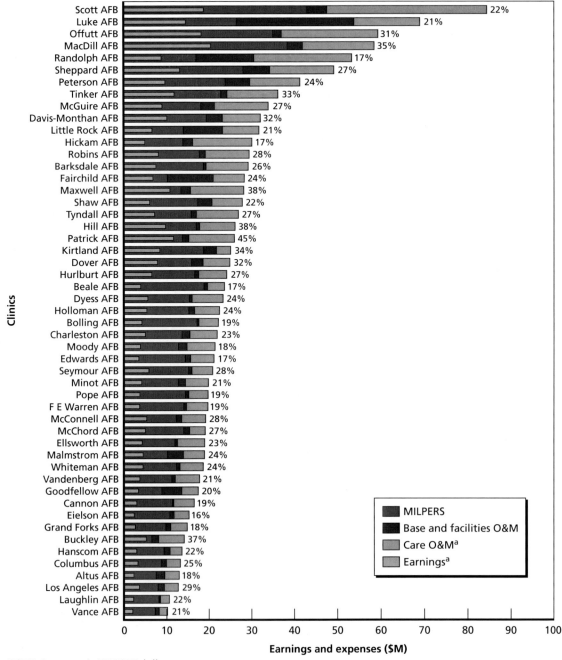

NOTE: Amounts in FY 2007 dollars.
[a] *Excluding* prescription ingredients.

question to ask is how AFMS's earnings compare to those of the Army and Navy medical services. This question is also relevant in light of the increasing costs of health care in the United States, as well as the growing burden of health-care benefits on the overall DoD budget. Such a comparison could shed light on whether all DoD medical services are inherently more expensive than civilian health care because of the inefficiencies of military health care or whether AFMS is inherently and uniquely less efficient because of its MTF structure and locations.

Methodology of the Medical Department Comparisons

To better understand how the economics of AFMS MTFs compare with those of Army and Navy MTFs, we analyzed the MTF expenses of all three services using reported costs for FY 2007 from the MEPRS data and earnings from PPS and MERHCF.[22] Our methodology in this section differs in three ways from the AFMS results shown previously. First, MEPRS is a DoD-wide cost-collection system that has been used to report annual expenditures, not just obligations (as used previously), since 1985.[23] Using data on MEPRS expenditures rather than obligations should not unfairly influence cross-service comparisons because the services should all be recording costs using OASD(HA) MEPRS guidance. Second, local MTF reimbursements (receipts from insurance companies, etc.) are reported as expenses in MEPRS because the money collected is money an MTF spends. However, because MEPRS does not include data on earnings and because we did not have data on obligations and local reimbursements for the Army and Navy, we compared MEPRS expenses to PPS and MERHCF earnings for all three services. This approach should not create any comparative bias unless local reimbursements were particularly high or low at one service's MTFs. It will understate earnings for all services. Finally, MEPRS costs include depreciation of capital equipment, which may have been procured in FY 2007 or earlier years. This depreciation would tend to increase MEPRS costs for all three services, and, again, was not considered a source of bias. Partly because we included depreciation, the reported costs for AFMS are higher in MEPRS than in the obligation-based data we used in the previous section.

Comparison of Medical Departments' Expenses and Earnings

Our analysis comparing the aggregate earnings and expenses for the three services' CONUS MTFs (again, CONUS in this context includes Alaska and Hawaii, but not overseas MTFs) suggests that the AFMS MTFs earn less as a percentage of their costs than Army or Navy MTFs do. Figure 3.6 shows the total expenses reported in MEPRS for each service, along with their earnings from PPS and MERHCF (excluding prescription ingredient costs). Whereas the Army and Navy medical services earn 58 and 51 percent of their expenses, respectively, AFMS earns only 46 percent of its total expenses.

---

[22] This report compares the earnings and operating expenses of MTFs. Comparing the financial performance of MTFs would require more-detailed analyses comparing specific types of workloads, specialty care offered, populations, etc.

[23] An obligation occurs when funds are placed on a contract, supplies are ordered, etc. An expenditure follows the obligation and occurs when the delivery under the contract occurs, an invoice is submitted by the provider of the good or service, and a payment is made by check or electronic funds transfer. Thus, an obligation might occur in one FY, but the related expenditure could occur in the following FY. We assume that, in a period of stable budgets, capturing expenditures (as MEPRS does) instead of obligations should allow for fair comparability across the service MTFs as residual expenditures from the previous year should be about the same year to year.

Figure 3.6
MEPRS Expenses Versus MERHCF and PPS Earnings in CONUS, by Service

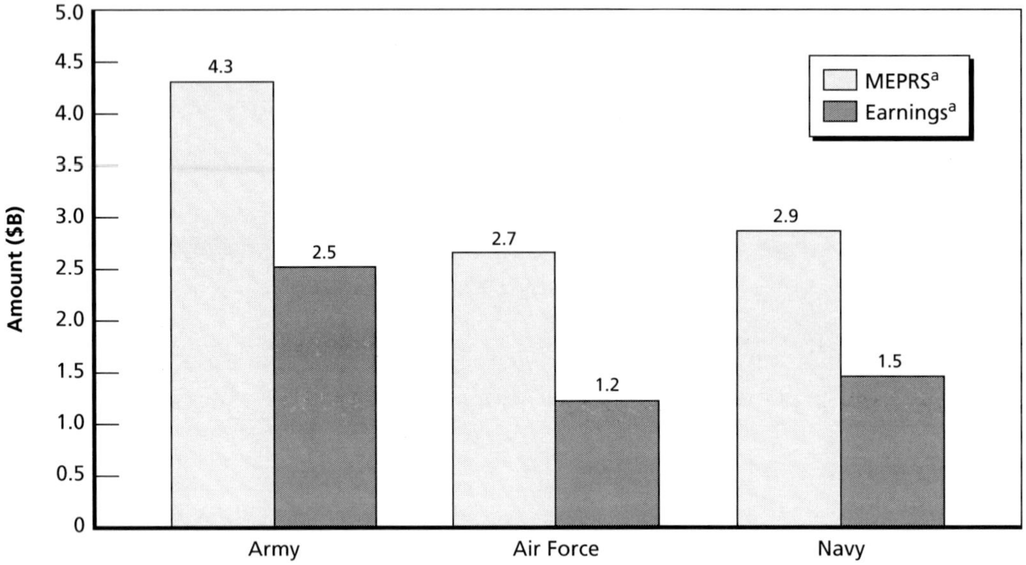

NOTES: The AFMS earnings shown here and those in Figure 3.1 differ because this figure excludes local reimbursements. Amounts in FY 2007 dollars.
[a] *Excluding* prescription ingredients.
RAND *TR859-3.6*

Prescription Costs

As noted in the efficiency-wedge section, MHS has a comparative advantage for lower prescription-ingredient costs than civilian pharmacies because of its participation in the federal ceiling price policy, which guarantees the lowest pharmaceutical prices to government entities. However, our comparisons of MTF expenses and earnings exclude prescription costs because, as stated previously, they are pass-through costs to each MTF. MTFs that dispense more prescriptions earn more (based on the costs of operating their pharmacies) under MERHCF, which we included in earnings. Figure 3.7 shows the CONUS MTF prescription costs and earnings by service. The figure compares the cost of prescriptions issued for active-duty and dependent beneficiaries to those for Medicare-eligible beneficiaries.

A case could be made that the greater the number of prescription ingredients issued at MTFs, the greater the savings to DoD because TRICARE would avoid having to pay for prescriptions filled at presumably more expensive civilian pharmacies.[24] This cost avoidance could be included in MTF earnings, but we had no analytical means of calculating or attributing such theoretical savings to each MTF; prices at civilian pharmacies could vary widely, depending on local network participation, competition, and other factors.[25]

---

[24] Assuming, again, that the relative pricing advantage for the MTFs holds true and that their operating costs are similar to those of civilian pharmacies.

[25] In addition, such savings calculations would have to assume that there was no change in demand between free prescriptions at an MTF and those requiring a copayment at a civilian pharmacy.

Figure 3.7
Comparison of Total Prescription Ingredient Expenses with MERHCF Earnings in CONUS, by Service

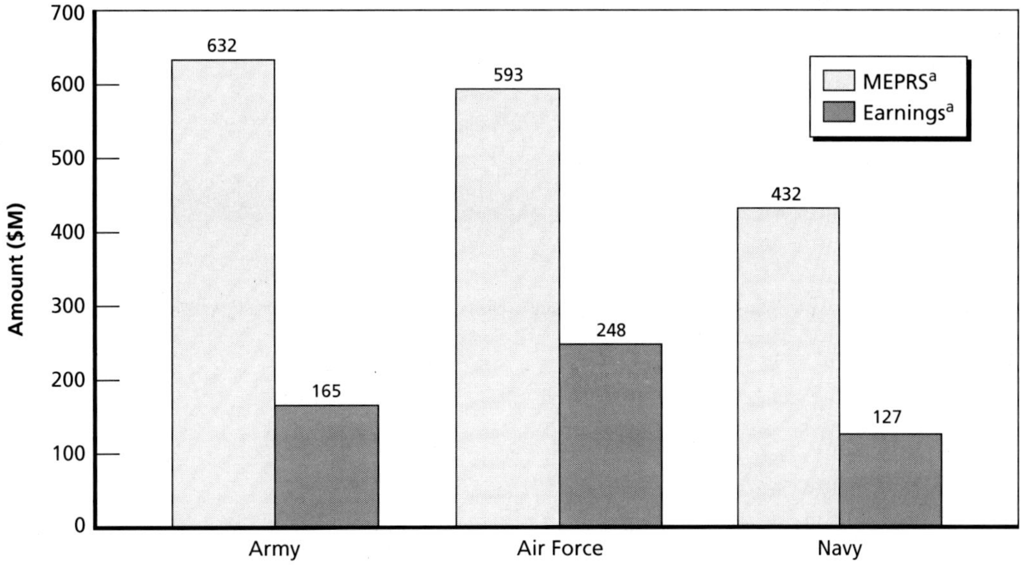

NOTE: Amounts in FY 2007 dollars.
[a]*Including* prescription ingredients.
RAND TR859-3.7

Comparing MTF Size and Earnings Share Across Services

In general, as the operating costs of the MTF decrease, its earnings also decrease. Thus, if one were to design a military health-care system based on efficiency alone, creating large MTFs with large patient populations and large inpatient workloads would produce the best results. As discussed in Chapter Two, the operational necessity of providing health care to the military population does not always allow the most efficient selection of MTF size, population, and workload. Thus, to serve its operational customers, AFMS operates stand-alone MTFs at virtually all Air Force bases that have relatively small beneficiary populations.[26]

In contrast to Table 2.2, which shows numbers for all medical centers, hospitals, and clinics by service, PPS reporting data consistently cover far fewer MTFs ("parents") in the Army and Navy and inconsistently cover geographically separate clinics ("children"). For example, even though the Army has 170 health-care facilities, it does not report earnings separately for all. A similar situation exists for the Navy. To be consistent in our comparison across services, we used reporting as documented at the parent MTFs, some of which may actually have several smaller clinics reporting workloads and data to them in the Army and Navy.

When we grouped the reporting MTFs in each service by size, based on their costs reported in MEPRS, we found that AFMS has more smaller stand-alone ("parent") clinics than the Army and Navy (see Table 3.2). Table 3.2 also shows earnings as a percentage of costs and the number of MTFs in each grouping. The table also shows that earnings as a percentage of operating costs vary by size and service, but no one service appears to be more or less efficient in all categories.

---

[26] Appendix A supplies the actual data for each MTF by service.

Table 3.2
Average PPS and MERHCF Earnings Share and Number of MTFs,
by MEPRS Expense Peer Grouping

Cost of MTF ($M)	Measure	Air Force	Army	Navy
<25	Earnings in relation to costs (%)	19	31	26
	MTFs in peer group (no.)	26	1	2
25–50	Earnings in relation to costs (%)	22	26	31
	MTFs in peer group (no.)	21	6	4
50–100	Earnings in relation to costs (%)	32	32	25
	MTFs in peer group (no.)	8	8	6
100–200	Earnings in relation to costs (%)	49	44	37
	MTFs in peer group (no.)	5	8	5
>200	Earnings in relation to costs (%)	59	59	54
	MTFs in peer group (no.)	2	8	4

NOTE: *Excluding* the costs of prescription ingredients.

Stepped-Down MEPRS A and B Expenses Versus Earnings

The comparisons between services shown in Figures 3.6 and 3.7 included all expenses reported in MEPRS, including those for dental care and readiness activities. In this section, we limit our analysis to expenses that are linked with patient medical care (inpatient and ambulatory care only).

For this, we used the "stepped-down" MEPRS A and B accounts as a measure of expenses; these accounts combine direct and indirect expenses for inpatient and outpatient care.[27] Figure 3.8 provides a comparison of the services' stepped-down CONUS MEPRS A and B expenses with their earnings, both excluding prescription costs.

For all hospitals and clinics, PPS and MERHCF earnings as a percentage of direct and indirect patient costs are 77 percent for the Army, 70 percent for the Air Force, and 69 percent for the Navy. However, separating hospitals and clinics into peer groupings based on MEPRS A and B costs shows a very high level of earnings at the major medical centers and lower earnings at smaller MTFs (see Table 3.3).

Table 3.3, like Table 3.2, shows that earnings as a percentage of operating costs vary by service and size of MTF, but no one service appears to earn more or less as a percentage of costs in all categories. However, the largest MTFs recover between 80 and 100 percent—or more in one case—of the cost of their medical care operations.

Future Military Health System Funding Concerns

Almost all interviewees for this study admitted that the most pressing MHS problems were not a function of insufficient funding. MHS received strong funding support from the Bush administration and Congress in a concerted effort to provide quality medical care to the armed

---

[27] Chapter Four explains how to calculate stepped-down MEPRS expenses. Appendix A shows stepped-down data by MTF.

Figure 3.8
Comparison of Stepped-Down CONUS MEPRS A and B Expenses with MERHCF and PPS Earnings, by Service

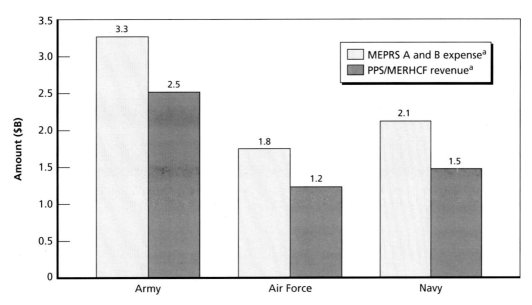

NOTE: Amounts in FY 2007 dollars.
[a] *Excluding* prescription ingredients.
RAND *TR859-3.8*

Table 3.3
Average PPS and MERHCF Earnings Share of Stepped-Down MEPRS A and B, and Number of MTFs, by MEPRS A and B Expense Peer Grouping

Cost of MTF ($M)	Measure	Air Force	Army	Navy
<25	Earnings in relation to costs (%)	56	50	45
	MTFs in peer group (no.)	48	7	5
25–50	Earnings in relation to costs (%)	49	53	47
	MTFs in peer group (no.)	4	6	6
50–100	Earnings in relation to costs (%)	60	59	55
	MTFs in peer group (no.)	7	6	4
100–200	Earnings in relation to costs (%)	99	71	58
	MTFs in peer group (no.)	2	8	3
>200	Earnings in relation to costs (%)	89	96	83
	MTFs in peer group (no.)	1	4	3

NOTE: *Excluding* the costs of prescription ingredients.

forces during the GWOT. Supplemental funding to the DHP has been significant each year, exceeding $1 billion in FYs 2007 and 2008. In addition, savings have been found within MHS, especially in the pharmacy area, that have been used to offset other costs. But, as noted in the MHS documentation sent to Congress with the FY 2009 President's Budget, there is concern about increasing health-care costs:

With the many benefit enhancements, increased beneficiary use, stable cost shares, and high healthcare inflation, the DoD's total health costs have more than doubled in five years, from $19 billion in 2001 to $38 billion in 2006, and now represent 8 percent of the DoD budget. Trend analysis projects that these costs will reach $64 billion, or 11.3 percent of the DoD budget by FY 2015. (DHP, undated, p. 4)

In addition, ASD(HA), under the President's Management Plan Performance Metrics Requirements, is committed to five performance measures and goals related to efficiency and effectiveness and has consistently pressed the services' medical activities to improve their efficiency in the foreseeable future.[28] AFMS, in terms of the visibility of its overall MTF earnings relative to its operating costs, is in the least advantageous position, partly because of its large number of stand-alone MTFs, which earn less efficiently than larger MTFs. Although PPS reductions have been modest thus far and although the efficiency wedge appears to be a one-year phenomenon, the possibility of larger earnings-based AFMS budget reductions looms in the future, especially in a post-GWOT environment.

However, a broader question is how efficient MHS can become. Given the ratios of earnings to operating expenses, it seems impossible to eliminate all non–workload-based subsidies to MTF operations, no matter how much more work is accomplished or how much more efficient the MTFs become. In addition, unless a major doctrinal change is made, health care—at least for active-duty personnel and their dependents—must continue to be provided at all locations where military personnel are stationed, regardless of MTF efficiencies.

Summary

This chapter described AFMS's funding and the components of its budget; compared operating expenses with earnings for the three services; and showed differences in earnings between larger hospitals and smaller, stand-alone clinics. We noted that AFMS may be at a disadvantage compared to the Army and Navy because it has a larger number of stand-alone MTFs, which, by their nature, earn smaller percentages of their operating costs. We also noted that, despite the trend toward allocating MHS funding based on documented and forecast workloads, a large portion of the MHS budget must still be justified by nonworkload factors. In the next chapter, we will examine how workloads are recorded and costs are collected in the MHS reporting systems.

---

[28] The five measures are beneficiary satisfaction, inpatient production, outpatient production, primary care productivity, and medical cost per member per year.

CHAPTER FOUR

Measuring Military Medical Service Costs and Workloads

Introduction

In evaluating MTF performance, we considered both the level of output and the resources used to produce that output. The predominant focus of the direct-care system is to improve health outcomes for individual patients and the overall population, meet access-to-care commitments, and advance patient satisfaction with the direct-care system. However, economics require serious consideration when assessing the long-term viability of MHS and its components, including AFMS. Holding health outcomes and military readiness constant, a more-efficient MTF is one that produces more output with a given set of inputs.

One primary output of an MTF is the patient care—what we have referred to as the workload—it provides to active-duty personnel, retirees, dependents, survivors, and certain other eligible beneficiaries.[1] As in the private sector, the quantity of inpatient medical care is measured by relative weighted products (RWPs); that of ambulatory care is measured using relative value units (RVUs).

Other outputs of an MTF include prescriptions filled, dental services, bioenvironmental services, and public health services for the installation population at large.

As we discussed in Chapter One, the clinical currency of the medical staff, military force readiness, and a healthy beneficiary population are the desired outcomes of the provision of health care.

The inputs to an MTF are the resources necessary to produce outputs: manpower, facilities, maintenance, supplies, etc.[2] These resource costs are dominated by the cost of military and civilian labor, which constitutes about 70 percent of the operating costs of a typical MTF. Manpower is measured in terms of the number of full-time equivalents (FTEs) (basically, FTEs) that are available at the MTF.

For a proper understanding of the performance of MTFs and of AFMS as a whole, it is vital to properly account for both the amount of patient care that MTFs provide and the costs incurred in the process. OASD(HA) monitors the amount of patient care provided by MTFs and uses the data to determine more than 30 percent of the AFMS medical budget. Furthermore, the relative efficiency of MTFs in producing that care is one basis of comparison within each military service, among the military services, and against purchased private-sector care.

---

[1] As defined in Title 10, U.S. Code.

[2] At the MHS level, other critical inputs include training, research, development, education, testing, and evaluation. We did not, however, consider these factors as direct inputs into MTF-level productivity for this report.

In addition to the budget implications of workload reporting, the prestige, reputation, and viability of the medical departments depend on getting proper credit for work performed.

In this chapter, we examine the systems that record the quantities and costs of inputs MTFs use and those that record the amount and value of work produced. We look at areas in which data may be inaccurate, distorted, difficult to measure or identify, or otherwise misleading. We examine the effects of these data problems on the measures used to judge performance and determine funding.

Reporting and Measuring Resources: Labor and Labor Costs

DoD uses MEPRS for standard reporting of all costs MTFs incur in providing patient care and other health-related support.[3] Only work and costs from fixed MTFs are reported in MEPRS, an issue that will be discussed later in greater detail. MEPRS is not a single piece of hardware or software. Rather, it is a cost collection, allocation, and reporting system that ties together data from three areas: manpower (personnel) data, financial data, and workload data. Unlike medical recording and accounting systems in the private sector, this is not an accounting or billing system, and it does not track monetary or labor costs as they occur for assignment to individual patients or specific services. MEPRS aggregates costs at the clinic (department) level in an MTF, assigning total recorded costs to broad categories.[4] It then computes average costs for different types of patient care or support services. Figure 4.1 shows the data inputs and flows in MEPRS.

Manpower is the primary input at MTFs. It is measured by the number of labor hours all personnel work (military, civilian, or contractor) to provide direct patient care, supply support functions, or engage in military duties not related specifically to patient care. All the services use the same personnel reporting system—the Defense Medical Human Resources System–Internet (DMHRSi)—to record these data. While actual costs for civilian employees and contractor personnel are recorded in MEPRS, composite costs by rank are used for military personnel.

Financial data are the second input to MEPRS, and, again, the services have different systems to account for costs. Expenses are tracked in AFMS by the Commander's Resource Integration System, in the Navy by the Standardized Accounting and Reporting System–Field Level, and in the Army by the Standard Finance System.

Workload is the output an MTF's medical staff produces. The medical care produced in all DoD fixed-facility MTFs is captured by the Composite Health Care System (CHCS). Inpatient care at an MTF is measured in RWPs, and ambulatory care is measured in RVUs. Both systems are described in more detail in the following section. CHCS captures detailed information on ambulatory care; in contrast, MEPRS captures the number of visits, which is a less informative measure of workload.[5] For inpatient care, MEPRS tracks admissions, occupied bed days, and dispositions.

---

[3] See DoD 6015.1-M, 1999, for a detailed explanation of MEPRS.

[4] Some interviewees suggested that, despite DoD-wide guidance, the allocation of common nonmanpower costs (such as military base security and maintenance) at MTFs could be inconsistent across facilities and services.

[5] The workload resulting from one visit to an MTF can vary widely, depending on the scope and complexity of the work done. One visit for a fairly simple matter might yield only a fraction of an RVU, while a more-complicated visit could result in more than one RVU.

Figure 4.1
Data Flows and Sources for MEPRS

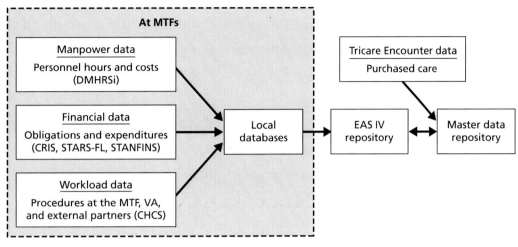

RAND *TR859-4.1*

MEPRS is a means of allocating manpower and other costs to a set of cost centers. Costs are initially assigned to a set of accounts, each corresponding to a work center or activity. Each account falls under one of seven broad categories:

A. Inpatient Care
B. Ambulatory (outpatient) Care
C. Dental Care
D. Ancillary Services—those that help providers care for patients rather than provide primary care (e.g., pharmacy, radiology, and intensive care)
E. Support Services—the nonmedical services that support care (e.g., depreciation; command, management, and administration; laundry; housekeeping; equipment repair; and supply)
F. Special Programs—health-related functions other than care of patients (e.g., public health, education, patient transport, and support to other agencies or other services' MTFs)
G. Readiness—military readiness functions that MTF personnel perform (e.g., military training, exercises, and deployments).

The information recorded in these MEPRS categories can be used to produce cost reports that can enable comparisons across MTFs and across services and, in theory, can also allow comparisons with private-sector care (although the latter claim is somewhat specious, given limitations we will describe later).

To produce better estimates of the total cost of medical and dental care, special programs, and readiness activities, MEPRS allocates personnel and other costs in shared functions, and the costs in the Ancillary (D) and Support (E) accounts (as recorded by the manpower and financial systems) to the other five cost accounts (called final operating expense accounts)—A, B, C, F, and G—based on the workloads recorded in the CHCS workload system (described in the next section).

Limitations in Reporting Manpower

There is a great deal of concern among OASD(HA) and AFMS personnel about the inaccuracy of data in MEPRS, particularly the manpower (labor hours) data. MEPRS depends on MTF personnel accurately filling out their timecards, which record the daily number of labor hours worked in each of the seven activities. Activities directly related to inpatient, outpatient, or dental care would be charged to three- or four-digit accounts starting with A, B, or C, respectively. Time spent in military and readiness activities would be charged to either F or G accounts. The latter two categories provide personnel (primarily military medical personnel) a way to account for the time they spend on activities that take them away from patient care. In theory, segregating the costs of the last two categories (F and G) should enable MTFs to track time available to be spent on patient care more accurately (categories A, B, or C) and, specifically, to measure the costs of providing health care more accurately.

However, interviews suggested that, in practice, timekeeping accuracy has not been a priority at MTFs. Although personnel are supposed to record their time accurately each day, interviewees reported that many medical personnel sign and submit their timecards only once every four weeks. Consequently, timesheets likely are not filled out until they are due (e.g., monthly), by which time personnel may have forgotten to record any nonclinical activities in which they had participated during the month.[6] Personnel at some MTFs are given templates with their most commonly used account codes to follow as an aid to filling out their timesheets, but this approach still requires personal record-keeping discipline to input actual time spent in both template and nontemplate activities.

Some interviewees reported a tendency for some MTF staff to fill out their timesheets with "Crazy 8s," i.e., they allocate eight hours per day every day to the same account codes. As a result, time spent on activities outside their primary assignment area or spent on other military or readiness activities is most likely not recorded accurately, and more time is reported on clinical work than on readiness or administrative duties. Other interviewees familiar with MEPRS and the analysis of the data felt these concerns were overblown and had been statistically disproven over time. To the extent that these practices do occur, the effect would be to reduce the apparent efficiency of the MTF, because extra hours are billed to patient care. Although timesheets are reviewed at the MTFs before submission, these reviews are normally done by timekeepers or administrative personnel, who ensure completeness, general accuracy for legitimate time codes, and other administrative details, rather than by supervisors, who would be more likely to know whether employees had actually worked the hours in the areas recorded and whether they had accurately recorded nonclinical duties.[7] Some anecdotes also suggest differences in local MTF policies on MEPRS reporting (i.e., some commanders cap reported time by military personnel at 40 hours per week, while others allow reporting of actual hours worked).[8]

---

[6]   With the implementation of DMHRSi in 2009, biweekly timecards are now required.

[7]   One exception to this pattern (based on interviews) may be the capturing of deployed FTEs. Part of the outprocessing actions for a person going on a temporary duty assignment would be to code that person as deployed (G coded) for the duration of the temporary assignment.

[8]   This generally would not be a problem with civilians or contractors because their hours in MEPRS must match actual paid hours.

Misreporting hours worked can affect the perceived efficiency of an MTF. Underreporting of actual hours would tend to increase the apparent efficiency of the MTF because overtime hours would not be charged to the workload. Misreporting among work centers within an MTF is relatively minor; it would affect only comparisons within an MTF or among similar work centers at different MTFs. A larger problem is misreporting the hours worked on patient care instead of readiness activities, for example, which could make some MTFs look more inefficient than others, to the extent that MTFs do not misreport uniformly.

It was unclear to us whether MTF personnel fully understand the implications of poor timekeeping on the metrics used to compare performance across MTFs and across services.[9] However, given that MEPRS is congressionally mandated and that the data are readily available for comparison (as in Chapter Five), it would seem important for the Air Force Surgeon General to reemphasize the need for AFMS personnel to report their time more accurately. AFMS should promote greater awareness and a better understanding of the importance of accurate timekeeping and the implications of these data for AFMS.[10]

Although concerns continue about the accuracy of timekeeping in AFMS, OSD began implementing a common personnel system, DMHRSi, across DoD. The system will enable easier and more accurate time reporting by MTF personnel through the use of an Internet-based timesheet, with templates for typical work locations and activities. Using DMHRSi, time reporting can be performed from any location, and reporting is required every two weeks, rather than monthly. The Army and Navy have fully implemented DMHRSi and AFMS transitioned to the new system in September 2009.[11] However, as with the older timekeeping system, individuals using DMHRSi will have to take responsibility for accurately reporting their time.

Reporting and Measuring Workload

Patient care is the primary output of an MTF, which means that measuring the patient care workload is essential for evaluating MTF performance. Accurate patient workload data affect this evaluation in many ways. From the physician's and patient's perspectives, these data are useful for clinical purposes, such as disease and case management. But the data are also used for MTF and MHS management because they populate metrics and inform decisions for PPS and MERHCF.[12]

CHCS, which documents medical encounters, is the original data-entry conduit for medical workload MHS MTFs produce. This initial source of workload documentation feeds both the Expense Assignment System Repository and the Master Data Repository. Data feeds that measure workload in MEPRS are typically unweighted workloads for visits and dispositions (and some weighted workloads for ancillary services, such as laboratory and x-ray). CHCS also populates Standard Ambulatory Data Records (SADRs) and Standard Inpatient Data Records

---

[9] Which we touched on in Chapter Three and will address again later in this chapter.

[10] Air Force policy changed on November 19, 2009, to require all MTF personnel to report actual hours. The Air Force's Assistant Surgeon General also made a point of stressing the importance of accurate reporting (Loftus, 2009).

[11] AFMS implemented DMHRSi on September 30, 2009.

[12] See Chapter Three for more on PPS and MERHCF and, respectively, Appendixes C and D.

(SIDRs) that, respectively, create RVUs and RWPs as weighted workload and are stored in the Master Data Repository.[13] CHCS does not capture important metrics associated with non-clinical work, including such military-unique readiness activities as physical fitness training, military predeployment training, or actual deployments. To the extent that one service or MTF engages in readiness efforts more heavily than others, these efforts will not be captured or receive credit if the metrics are not properly constructed or if the efforts (e.g., FTEs) are not accurately recorded in MEPRS.[14]

The following is a list of workloads captured in CHCS, with the corresponding MEPRS code:

- Inpatient Care (MEPRS A)
- Ambulatory Care (MEPRS B)
- Dental Care (MEPRS C)
- Ancillary Services (MEPRS D)
- Special Programs (MEPRS F).

A limitation of using only unweighted workload, such as visits, admissions, or days as output measures (as captured in MEPRS), is that these measures cannot account for variations in case mix and complexity that define the resources necessary to treat individual patients and their needs.

As Figure 4.1 showed, workload, financial, and personnel data are gathered at each MTF, consolidated in a local MTF database, and then sent on to the Expense Assignment System Repository, which stores all MEPRS data for all the services' MTFs. A parallel system produces the weighted workload. The weighted workload is used for such purposes as the PPS and MTF performance metrics (e.g., RVUs per provider FTE per day). Accurate clinical coding is the basis for calculating RWPs and RVUs because a standard resource-intensity measure is applied to each coded procedure.

These data systems are evolving. As with the effort to improve personnel data collection with DMHRSi, efforts to improve the accuracy of workload data collection are ongoing. DoD is moving toward a common electronic health record known as the Armed Forces Health Longitudinal Technology Application. It is intended to improve documentation of outpatient visits and will eventually encompass CHCS ancillary services. This application is expected to improve coding and documentation of patient visits through the use of structured notes with automated evaluation and management codes. The data will still be rolled up into current systems for overall workload measurement. MHS has also begun implementing an inpatient coding system to improve documentation services at the bedside.

As part of its effort to track workloads over time for individual MTFs and for the services, TMA also examines closed patient records. Open records are not included in the measures of RVUs and RWPs that MTFs produce and are therefore not included in earnings attributable

---

[13] CHCS does not capture purchased-care workloads or work done at other federal treatment facilities, although it does capture military provider professional services by using a special Defense Medical Information System (DMIS) identifier in the 2000 or 5400 series.

[14] ASD(HA) has sought to quantify these nonclinical, military-related activities in an ongoing initiative, the Mission Essential Non-Benefit Activities study, designed to document all military-unique activities at the MTFs to allow better comparability across services and with civilian health-care activities.

to MTFs. The data indicate that the services could do a more timely job of coding and closing cases, which is a basic administrative responsibility. Data provided to RAND indicated that AFMS lost over $8 million in FY 2007 earnings because of delays in closing SADRs. The Army and Navy had slightly larger lost earnings.

Limitations on Workload Reporting

As noted earlier, the current approach focuses on only one output—direct health care provided to beneficiaries at MTFs. There is no "output" measure for readiness and other nonclinical activities, although the number of hours (i.e., the input) devoted to these activities can be captured in the manpower systems.

Even within the context of health care, these systems do not capture all of MHS's output. The inpatient SIDR and ambulatory and outpatient SADR records capture only workload produced in fixed MTF facilities. The efforts of AFMS personnel deployed in theater, such as at Balad, Bagram, and other sites in Southwest Asia, are not captured for workload reporting purposes. While MEPRS can document the lack of availability of deployed staff, it does not explain a specific MTF's circumstances and consequently does not attribute an appearance of inefficiency to maintaining underutilized infrastructure while staff are deployed.

The current systems attribute workload to the site at which it was performed using a unique DMIS identifier for the MTF. If an Air Force physician provides care for a beneficiary at an Army MTF, that workload is attributed to the Army MTF. In addition, the Air Force physician should be picked up as borrowed military manpower within the Army MEPRS system. However, MEPRS aggregates all borrowed military manpower, so it is not possible to track the workload back to the provider's home organization. Thus, for example, the personnel costs associated with the AFMS personnel the Army borrows, if coded accurately, are charged to the Army through the borrowed military manpower coding.

On the positive side, this method properly attributes the costs of the work accomplished to the site that contributes the fixed and other support costs expended in producing the work if the borrowing site collects and reports the manpower costs in the relevant periods accurately. In addition, if the loaned personnel working outside their home MTF properly code their time as either "F" or "G," their home MTF patient care costs will not be negatively affected.

However, this approach masks the financial contributions of the parent military services of the loaned professionals that initially trained and supported the providers and that pay their salaries. Currently, it is not possible to disentangle the output of an individual provider from the site at which the work is performed. It is only possible to track the "borrowed" personnel as "available" to the recipient MTF, but this augmented manpower cannot be linked to a particular parent military service. As a result, the loaning military service loses workload credit and earnings under PPS or MERHCF (or, conversely, the gaining military service receives the workload credit and PPS or MERHCF earnings). The fixed costs of the loaning MTF are spread over a smaller workload, making the remaining workload appear more costly per unit. More importantly, the salaries of the loaned personnel are not reimbursed to the home service through PPS or MERHCF. To the extent that the services "borrow" equally from each other, this would not be a problem.

However, as Figure 4.2 shows, the Army is a much larger recipient of borrowed labor than the Navy or AFMS. The figures for officers in MEPRS categories A and B indicate that the Army borrowed about 600 FTE man-years of effort in FY 2007 in its inpatient and outpatient care operations at MTFs, whereas the Navy and AFMS borrowed less than 100 FTEs. Assum-

Figure 4.2
Borrowed Military Officer Manpower, by Service and Fiscal Year

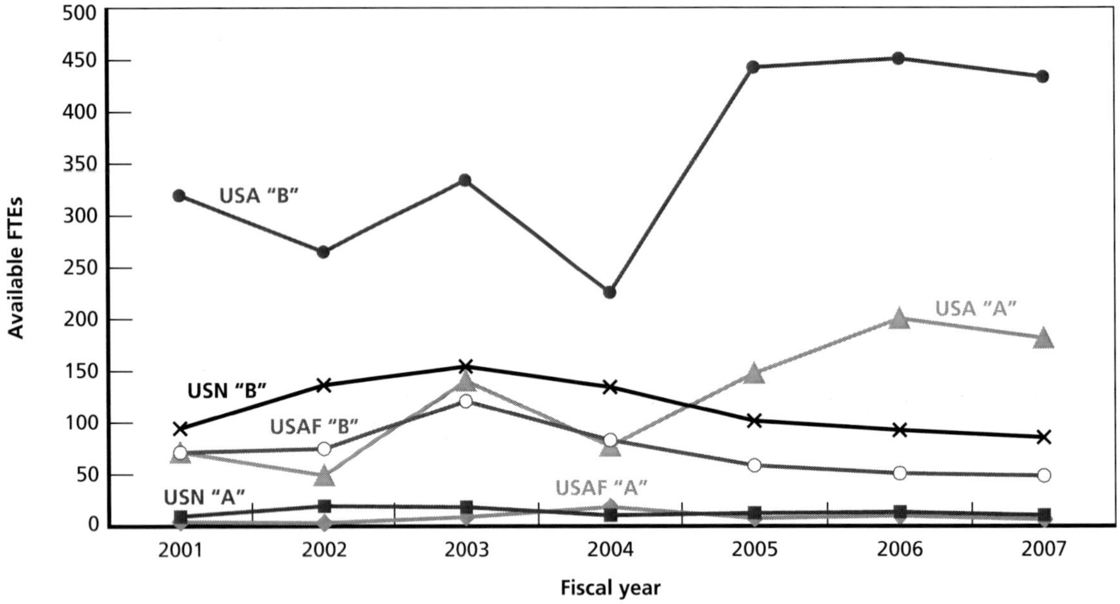

ing the output was roughly the same per FTE, PPS and MERHCF would overcompensate the Army and undercompensate the Navy and AFMS for the salaries of the loaned personnel. The variable support costs should generally be properly attributed, however, based on the workload accomplished at each location.

To help address the issue of uncredited workload, DoD is implementing a National Provider Identification (NPI) system to serve as a mechanism for identifying individual personnel across MTFs and services. Providers will be assigned a unique identifier that can also be applied to each patient encounter in which they participate. Using this identifier, the services and MHS will gain insight into their providers' contributions regardless of their assignment. We caution, however, that NPI is only a partial solution because it applies only to providers. It is not possible to track the contributions of certain support staff (e.g., nurses and technicians supporting providers) because they will not be given identification numbers.

Summary of Benefits

Tracking labor hours, costs, and outcomes is important to satisfy OASD(HA) efforts to manage resources effectively. For example, tracking the hours and workloads of AFMS personnel at non-AFMS facilities would allow an accurate assessment for TMA's PPS and efficiency metrics (e.g., total workload and RVUs per provider FTE per day). Combined with outcome data from the electronic medical record, this information may also help measure quality. Using DMHRSi and NPI to improve the accuracy of workload and manpower can be helpful both within MHS and for external partnerships and assignments at nonmilitary sites.[15]

---

[15] External partnerships are agreements between an MTF and a local civilian hospital or clinic that allow DoD providers to treat beneficiaries at the civilian facility. DoD gets credit and earnings for the professional portion of the work, and the civilian facility gets reimbursed for the institutional portion of the charge.

The ability to track the workloads of individual providers regardless of the site is becoming increasingly important for several reasons. First, the reorganization of CONUS MTFs has blurred the lines between military services in such areas as San Antonio and the National Capital Region. For example, in San Antonio, AFMS's WHMC and the Army's BAMC were in the process of integrating operations as the San Antonio Military Medical Center (SAMMC). Both MTFs will remain open but will operate as SAMMC South (WHMC) and SAMMC North (BAMC). Personnel will be assigned to either campus according to their specialties, which will be based at one of the campuses or both. Although specific MEPRS codes have been established for personnel to properly record their time at either facility, the merger of these two sites will make it difficult for AFMS and TMA to track AFMS work accomplished and the associated salaries without changing the current system. As stated previously, NPI will increase recognition of the providers' workload but not that of support staffs. Yet each service will have to pay the salaries of their own military and civilian employees, regardless of where they normally are assigned.[16]

How Do System Inaccuracies Affect Performance Measures and Funding?

The data collected in the systems described previously affect measures that are used to determine funding levels or to measure the performance of individual MTFs and the medical services as a whole. However, according to AFMS officials, there are three areas of possible concern:

- PPS
- primary care productivity
- MERHCF.

Prospective Payment System

PPS is one of the performance measurement tools OASD(HA) uses to incentivize health-care production by adjusting a portion of each military service's annual medical budget based on its workload.[17] Because PPS relies on CMAC rates, the actual costs the MTFs incur in providing care and report in MEPRS are irrelevant to earnings calculations and, therefore, to budget distributions. However, the work the MTFs accomplish and report is crucial to determining earnings for the military services' medical systems.

As stated previously, the inability of current systems to track the workload of AFMS providers working in non-AFMS facilities can cause workload of the loaning service to be underreported. That, in turn, means that the professional component of the earnings can be undercompensated if AFMS is a net provider of personnel to non-AFMS sites. In addition to the manpower loaned to other services' MTFs, for which workload credit is not received in

---

There are also efforts to create child DMIS identifiers for external sites to allow the services to track the non-MHS workload. These should be useful both for highlighting the workload but, in some cases, for obtaining partial reimbursement for the services these facilities provide DoD beneficiaries. See Chapter Six for more information on the possibilities for AFMS to increase cooperation with facilities outside the DoD system.

[16] See Appendix E for additional information on the SAMMC integration.

[17] See Chapter Three and Appendix C for more information on PPS. The topic is included here for context.

a budgetary sense, AFMS, like the other services, receives no credit for workload performed in nonfixed facilities (for example, in theater facilities in Southwest Asia and other deployed locations). In addition, unless Air National Guard, Air Force Reserve, civilian, or contractor personnel can fill in for these providers while they are deployed, there will be a net loss of workload, and therefore earnings, at the home MTFs. For example, about 60 surgeon FTEs (about 8 percent of all surgeons) in AFMS in FY 2007 were deployed away from their home MTFs.

In addition, some AFMS providers based at small MTFs lacking inpatient facilities have agreements with nearby civilian hospitals to use their facilities for DoD beneficiary patients, as external partnership arrangements. When the AFMS provider sees his or her patient in the civilian hospital, AFMS may not receive workload credit unless the provider conscientiously records his or her time and work.[18] This has the potential to understate the AFMS workload and reduce the funding provided under PPS or MERHCF.

As discussed earlier, this problem will be exacerbated when AFMS shares facilities with other federal agencies, such as the merger of WHMC in San Antonio with the nearby BAMC. If systems are not put in place to record the work AFMS providers performed in the shared SAMMC locations, AFMS will appear to have lost an entire inpatient hospital's workload (in fact, its largest single source), with significant consequences for AFMS funding if the new joint arrangement is not fully understood at the levels of the service surgeons general and OASD(HA).[19] Similar workload losses would result if AFMS increased its partnerships with civilian facilities (see Appendix G).

Primary Care Productivity

A second performance metric OASD(HA) uses to judge the efficiency of MTFs, primary care productivity, shows that AFMS providers are underperforming relative to the DoD-wide norm. Primary care productivity is a ratio: the number of RVUs per provider FTE per day for primary care.[20] The numerator of this ratio is the number of RVUs, a measure of the outpatient workload, which comes from the MHS Management Analysis and Reporting Tool. The denominator is the number of FTE providers recorded in MEPRS as being available at (rather than assigned to) the MTF's primary care unit (MEPRS B code). Thus, deployed personnel or those properly coded into MEPRS as participating in readiness or other activities would not adversely affect this metric.

According to OASD(HA), the average MHS provider FTE in FY 2007 produced 15.6 RVUs per day. However, the AFMS average was about 10 percent lower. The long-term goal of OASD(HA) is to meet the civilian sector benchmark, which is about 18.5 RVUs per day (about 25 visits per day).[21] In addition to physicians, providers can include nurse practitioners, physician assistants, psychologists, etc.

---

[18] The credit, however, should accrue only for the provider's time because the civilian hospital would be providing only the facility and support staff.

[19] WHMC accounts for about 25 percent of total AFMS earnings and almost 50 percent of its inpatient earnings.

[20] Primary Care Productivity is one of the five President's Management Plan Performance Metrics.

[21] A memorandum from OASD(HA) asserts that "[e]xperience from the civilian health-care sector indicates that 3 to 3.5 support staff per provider who are directly in the clinic is optimal for a patient throughput of 3.5 to 4 visits per hour" (Bailey, 2000, attachment). This would equate in an 8 hour day to 28 to 32 visits per provider per day. Murray, Davies, and Boushon, 2007, established an ideal workload of 24 visits per provider per day.

Clearly, the number of FTEs allocated to patient care (in this example, the MEPRS B account) will affect this metric, as will any inaccuracies in that allocation, as discussed earlier. For example, overreporting the number of hours considered available for clinical care because of inaccurate recording of time spent in readiness or other infrequent activities would depress the workload-to-provider FTE ratio. Inaccurately coding deployments or temporary assignments to other services' MTFs as time spent in the home clinic will also understate the RVUs per FTE metric. However, each service has the ability to ensure that the data reported in MEPRS are accurate, so comparisons with the other services can be accomplished with the appropriate data.

Regardless of the ability to backfill providers deploying or engaging in readiness activities, primary care workload per available FTE should not be affected because both the workload produced (numerator) and the number of providers available (denominator) should be equally affected, aside from "spin-up" time for an outside provider to be incorporated into an MTF.

Medicare-Eligible Retiree Health Care Fund

Unlike PPS, which uses CMAC rates to calculate earnings for the MHS direct-care workload, MERHCF uses the actual costs reported in MEPRS for its rates.[22] Hence, inaccuracies in MEPRS costs can directly affect earnings calculations and therefore the services' budgets. If MEPRS costs are overstated, the reimbursements will be higher than they should be. Assuming MEPRS reporting is accurate, MERHCF should have a neutral effect on services' current earnings, with earnings equal to actual expenses. Inaccuracies could have a larger negative effect on the accrual portion of MERHCF; if MEPRS costs are overstated, the MERHCF liability for future retirees will be higher than it should be, affecting many future years rather than just current earnings.[23] Overstating MEPRS costs would adversely affect the calculation of the portion of the DoD budget allocated to the MERHCF accrual for many years. Thus, MEPRS cost inaccuracies not only would affect MHS directly and immediately but, as part of the accrual calculations, would also have longer-term implications for future DoD budgets.

Summary

Evaluating the performance of MHS in terms of costs and efficiency is a multifaceted undertaking. Unlike civilian institutions, whose primary focus is on providing health care at a specific location with a relatively stable workforce, the military medical system must not only provide patient health care at MTFs but also support many military-unique operational requirements, such as readiness training and deployments. These activities change the focus of health-care providers and staff from their day-to-day role, providing health care to beneficiaries, to their operational role (or training for it), providing medical care to deployed airmen and other members of the armed forces. The latter role reduces the clinical workload and the associated earnings for their MTFs under PPS and MERHCF. In addition, nonfinancial assessments, such as primary care productivity, are also used to measure MTF and service performance.

---

[22] See Chapter Three and Appendix D for more information on MERHCF.

[23] See Appendix D for an explanation.

Over the years, OASD(HA) has attempted to gather uniform reporting from the three military services and to incentivize efficient workload production. Initiated in 1985, MEPRS was an early, congressionally mandated initiative to tie together various component systems and produce comparable data on the cost of health care. More recently, such new initiatives as DMHRSi and NPI have been proposed to improve the accuracy and scope of health-care reporting.

Despite these improved systems and the fact that MTFs have to certify that there are no process issues with their monthly data submissions, many interviewees expressed concerns about the accuracy of the data, variations in implementation across the military services, the level of detail, and the ability to capture all relevant aspects of performance. Not surprisingly, there are concerns about whether the data available are appropriate to determining funding levels and for supporting other MHS health-care management decisions.

CHAPTER FIVE

Why Has the Air Force Medical Service's Workload Decreased?

A challenge for AFMS has been maintaining a stable workload base in its clinics and hospitals. As we will show in more detail later, Air Force workload decreased substantially from FY 2000 to FY 2007.[1] Indeed, in FY 2007, AFMS performed 37 percent fewer inpatient procedures and conducted 31 percent fewer outpatient visits than in FY 2000 and filled 11 percent fewer prescriptions than in FY 2002.[2] These workload reductions have resulted in decreased DHP funding for the Air Force, which negatively affects the available resources, financial health, and management flexibility of AFMS. In addition, decreased funding also affects nonfinancial considerations, such as the reputation and perception of AFMS as a viable full-service medical department.

This chapter examines the likely causes of the decreased workload, including both directly quantifiable causes and other, underlying factors. The purpose of this evaluation is not only to document these changes but also to determine where future efforts can be made to restore the workload, especially after the GWOT requirements decrease. Workload restoration is vital to AFMS currency, budget allocations, and overall perceptions about its role as an MHS health-care activity.

Although we examined all types of AFMS workloads, we focused on the inpatient workload for two reasons. First, as shown in Chapter Three, an inpatient procedure (admission to a hospital) produces about 150 times the earnings of an ambulatory procedure and thus has a much greater effect on the AFMS budget.[3] Second, the training and currency of critical-care specialists (such as surgeons, operating room and intensive care nurses, and technicians), who have been in high demand during the GWOT, are more closely associated with the inpatient workload.

In the next section, we estimate the contributions of several factors to the decrease in the AFMS inpatient workload from FY 2000 to FY 2007: the effects of readiness activities, especially deployments; the number of surgeons available each year; the conversion of ten AFMS hospitals to stand-alone clinics or ASCs; TFL implementation;[4] and the damage to Keesler

---

[1] FY 2000 was the last "peacetime" fiscal year preceding the GWOT and was thus a good baseline year for comparison.

[2] Because of data availability, we measured prescriptions from an FY 2002 baseline.

[3] Inpatient procedures also cost more to produce, although a large part of that expense is relatively fixed in the short term (personnel, equipment and facility depreciation, etc.). Using a rule of thumb of $72 for an ambulatory visit and $11,825 per inpatient procedure from PPS reimbursement rates, lost ambulatory workload cost AFMS $216 million annually in FY 2007; the inpatient workload lost was about $260 million. These losses would be greater using MERHCF rates, which are based on actual costs incurred at the MTFs.

[4] See Appendix D for an explanation of TFL.

AFB hospital due to Hurricane Katrina. Finally, we examine how well AFMS has been able to find substitutes for deployed providers and nurses to meet MTF workload demands.

Work Accomplished, FYs 2000–2007

Since FY 2000, there has been a major shift in DoD's health-care workload from direct to purchased care. Between FY 2000 and FY 2007, the overall DoD inpatient workload increased by 19 percent, primarily because purchased care increased dramatically, with 52 percent more RWPs in FY 2007 than in FY 2000. At the same time, the Air Force and Navy workloads decreased, and the Army's increased slightly. Figure 5.1 shows the RWPs of the three services and the RWPs purchased at civilian institutions from FY 2000 through FY 2007.

This workload shift reinforces the OSD push to use work accomplished as one of the methodologies for distributing funding.[5]

During the same period, the overall ambulatory workload grew by 30 percent, while the AFMS workload decreased by 31 percent and the Navy's dropped by 11 percent. The Army's direct-care workload grew slightly, while the number of purchased care visits increased by 98 percent. Figure 5.2 shows the ambulatory workload for FYs 2000 through 2007. To complete the picture, Figure 5.3 displays prescriptions for the same period.

Figure 5.1
Inpatient Relative Weighted Products for the DoD Population, FYs 2000–2007

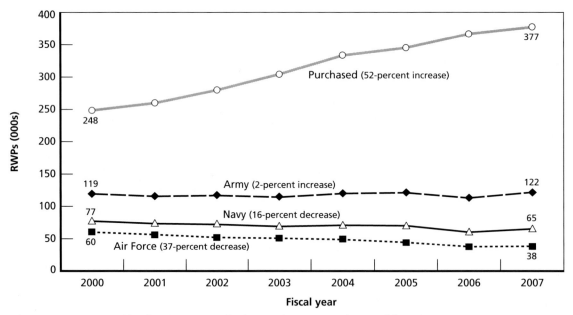

SOURCE: Data extracted by the Air Force Medical Operations Agency (AFMOA) for RAND.
RAND *TR859-5.1*

---

[5] Workload-based funding is seen as a means of eliminating what could be considered a double payment from TMA: Either the services should perform the workload for which they are funded, or, if the workload was purchased outside the MTFs, their budgets should be decreased. Linking workload to budgets was considered a means of either incentivizing the services to increase their workload (and avoid payments for purchased care by TRICARE) or reducing their costs.

Figure 5.2
Ambulatory Visits for the DoD Population, FYs 2000–2007

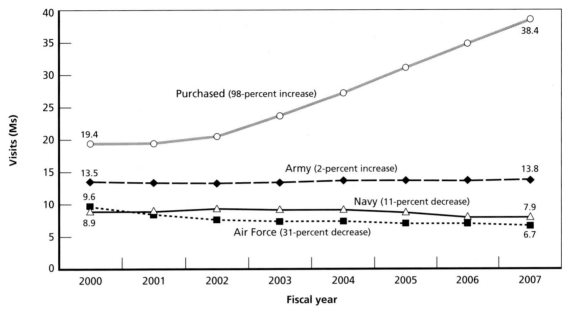

SOURCE: Data extracted by AFMOA for RAND.
RAND *TR859-5.2*

Figure 5.3
Prescriptions Filled, FYs 2002–2007

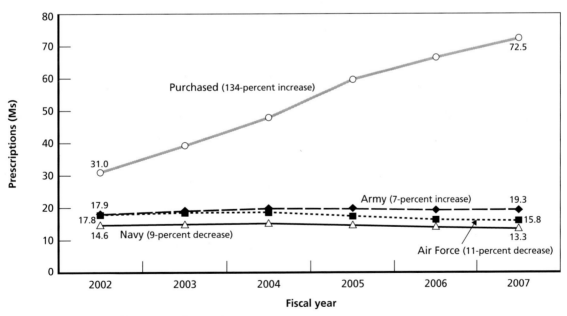

SOURCE: Data extracted by AFMOA for RAND.
RAND *TR859-5.3*

During the five-year period, total prescriptions filled increased by 49 percent, largely driven by a 134-percent increase in purchased prescriptions. AFMS and Navy prescriptions were down, while Army prescriptions increased slightly.[6]

In the next sections, we will systematically examine factors that might explain these decreases. First, we will examine readiness and deployment activities during the decade and then evaluate other possible causes.

Effects of Readiness and Deployments on Workload Production

Immediately following the 9/11 attacks, the operational tempo of all the military services and their medical components increased dramatically. To portray that activity, we extracted data from MEPRS to examine the allocation of work hours among the various MEPRS categories. Medical personnel logging their time in readiness activities (G codes) would not be performing duties related to direct workload production or support in the inpatient or outpatient activities of their home-station MTFs. Our primary interest was in the amount of time AFMS devoted to readiness activities changed from FY 2000 to FY 2007 and in comparing that with the other services over the same period to see whether this was a possible explanation for AFMS workload reductions.

We gathered data from MEPRS (discussed at length in Chapter Four). First, we gathered data on total FTEs by service and by category.[7] Table 5.1 shows all FTEs the three services recorded in the seven basic categories for FY 2007 only: Inpatient, Outpatient (ambulatory), Dental, Ancillary, Support, Special, and Readiness.

The Air Force recorded a higher percentage of its available FTEs in the Readiness account than did the Army or the Navy.[8] The table shows the allocation of total FTEs and includes anyone assigned to an MTF: physicians, direct-care professionals, nurses, technicians, supply personnel, etc.

Table 5.1
Allocation of Available Time by MEPRS Category, FY 2007 (percent)

Service	Inpatient	Outpatient	Dental	Ancillary	Support	Special	Readiness
Army	7	25	6	17	28	12	5
Air Force	4	26	7	14	26	13	9
Navy	6	26	8	16	29	9	8

---

[6]   Data were available on service-filled prescriptions only from FY 2002 and later. Purchased prescription data were available from FY 2000, which showed that purchased prescriptions alone increased by 305 percent, from 14.3 million prescriptions in FY 2000 to 72.5 million in FY 2007.

[7]   FTE is a measure of the time spent in one year by one person, or 252 days (or one workyear). This is derived from the MEPRS system, which uses 168 hours per month as the availability of one person. We calculated the FTEs in these tables by multiplying the number of deployed persons, by specialty, times the number of deployed days and divided by 252.

[8]   According to DoD 6010.13-M, 2008, p. 168, par. C2.7.1: "The Readiness account summarizes the expenses of an MTF that are incurred as a result of performing the readiness portion of its military mission rather than direct patient care." This account is designed to collect the personnel time and costs spent on such activities as deployments, exercises, readiness training, and physical training.

Figure 5.4 illustrates the trend data for readiness FTEs in the three services since FY 2001. As shown, all three military services began with all medical personnel in readiness activities in FY 2001 recording similar levels of FTEs, but AFMS grew by a larger proportion (about 200 percent) than did the Army and Navy (about 85 percent each). In FY 2007, AFMS recorded the greatest number of readiness FTEs, despite it being the smallest medical service.

As noted in Chapter Two, one of the major differences among the services is the assignment of some of the enlisted technicians and medics to operational units in the Army and Navy, while they are assigned almost exclusively to MTFs in the Air Force (notable exceptions being squadron medical elements—flight surgeons and technicians assigned to flying units—and personnel assigned to the Air Force's four AE squadrons). Thus, a deploying technician or medic might not be recorded as a readiness cost for the Army or Navy if assigned to a line (nonmedical) unit because MEPRS captures only MTF costs, but such an individual would show up in Air Force MEPRS reporting as a readiness cost.

To overcome this problem, we examined Readiness FTEs and the FTEs recorded for deployments separately for clinicians (physicians, dentists, and veterinarians) and nurses.[9] As shown in Table 5.2, all services had significant increases in recorded Readiness FTEs for both clinicians and nurses between FYs 2001 and 2007. The growth in readiness FTEs for Air Force clinicians was three times that of the other two military services—an increase of 175 percent for AFMS compared to 59 percent for the Army and 57 percent for the Navy. For nurses, the Air Force reported more readiness FTEs than either the Navy or Army.

Figure 5.4
Available Readiness Full-Time Equivalents Recorded, FYs 2001–2007

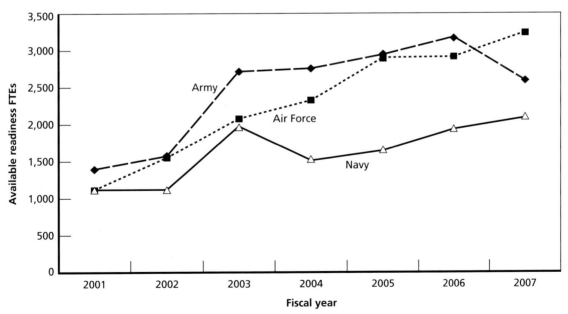

SOURCE: Data extracted by AFMOA for RAND.
RAND TR859-5.4

---

[9] The FTEs in the Clinician category are overwhelmingly for physicians. AFMS had no veterinarians and only 12 dentist FTEs deployed in FY 2007.

However, when we look at deployed FTEs of clinicians and nurses for the same period, we find significant increases for all services, with the Army having the most deployed clinicians and nurses of the three services. The percentage of the total Readiness FTEs identified as deployed FTEs shows the Air Force percentages for both groups being lower than the other two, although higher than the Navy in FTEs. It was beyond the scope of the project to determine how the nondeployed Readiness FTEs were spent.

The data in Tables 5.2 and 5.3 include all physicians recording readiness time in MEPRS, but we are interested in the economic effects of these lost work hours, especially on inpatient workload production. To examine these effects, we further focused our analysis on the number of surgeons available to perform inpatient workload.

Decline in the Number and Availability of Air Force Medical Service Surgeons

There has been a steady decrease in the total number of AFMS surgeons since FY 2000, as well as in their availability at their home MTFs. Barring some use of surgeons in other new roles, we would expect to find some relationship between the surgeons available and the inpatient workload.[10] Figure 5.5 shows the number of AFMS surgeons on active duty each year, which

Table 5.2
Increases in Annual Readiness FTEs, by Service, FYs 2001–2007

	Air Force			Army			Navy		
	2001	2007	Increase (%)	2001	2007	Increase (%)	2001	2007	Increase (%)
Clinicians	126	346	175	245	389	59	137	215	57
Nurses	77	250	225	85	237	179	101	157	55

NOTES: Appendix B contains more data on the deployment and nondeployment FTEs by service. In general, between 40 and 45 percent of clinician readiness FTEs were devoted to deployments; for nurses, the percentage was about 50 percent.

Table 5.3
Percentage Increase in Annual Deployed FTEs, by Service, FYs 2001–2007

	Air Force			Army			Navy		
	2001	2007	%	2001	2007	%	2001	2007	%
Clinicians									
Number	32	153		44	284		1	136	
Increase			378			545			13,500
Readiness FTEs (%)	25	44		18	73		1	63	
Nurses									
Number	11	132		11	173		0.4	105	
Increase			1,100			1,472			26,150
Readiness FTEs (%)	14	53		13	73		—	67	

---

[10] Because our focus was on the economics of AFMS, further dividing the inpatient workload into types of procedures and the specific clinical specialties that would likely perform each procedure would have been beyond the scope of this project.

Figure 5.5
Air Force Surgeon Full-Time Equivalents, Deployed and Nondeployed, FYs 2000–2007

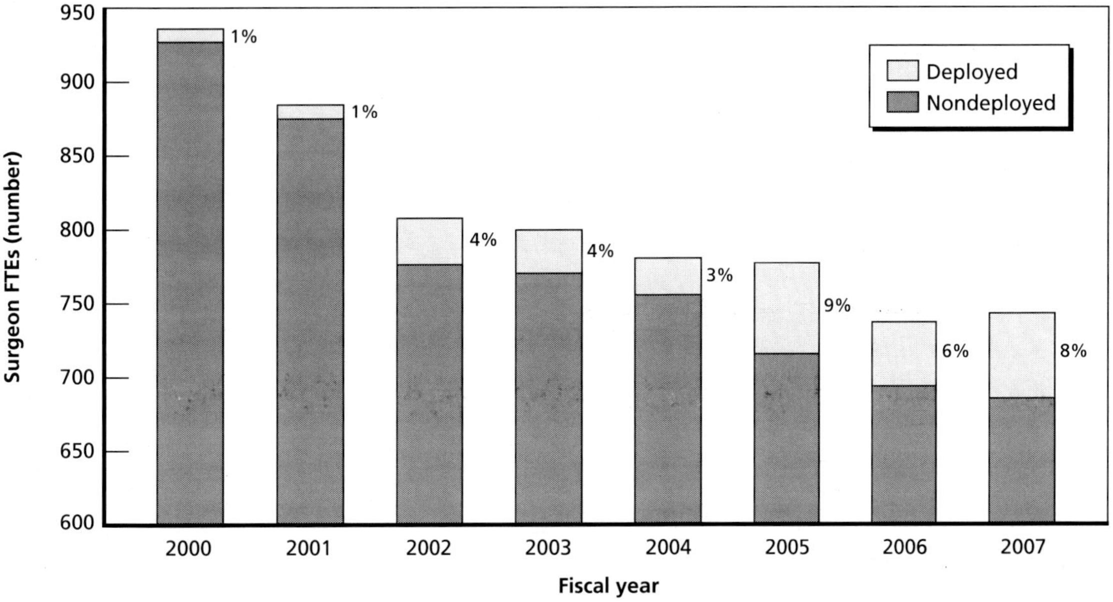

SOURCE: Data extracted by AFMOA for RAND.
RAND TR859-5.5

we equate to the number of FTEs. We also gathered actual deployment data for the surgeon Air Force Specialty Codes (AFSCs) and converted both into deployed and nondeployed FTEs, as shown later.[11]

The total number of AFMS surgeons (and therefore FTEs) decreased 21 percent between FYs 2000 and 2007 (from 936 to 743).[12] The number of surgeons deployed and therefore unavailable to produce inpatient workload increased by more than 400 percent (from 11 to 46 FTEs). As a result, the number of surgeons available to perform inpatient work at their MTFs decreased by 26 percent (from 927 to 686).[13] If data were available on work each deployed surgeon accomplished prior to deployment (for example, a monthly average of each surgeon's workload), more accurate losses of workload due to deployments could be estimated. However, such data are unavailable, so we present these data as one of several contributing factors to a decrease in overall inpatient workload.

---

[11] The Air Force Specialty for the general category of surgeons is 45XX, which is displayed in Figure 5.5.

[12] We obtained data on the number of deployed surgeons and the durations of their deployments, then converted the data into annual FTEs for each year. The remainder are nondeployed FTEs. Thus, in a single year, three surgeons might deploy for four months each, resulting in one deployed FTE. The intent is to show the equivalent lost workload by year due to deployments.

[13] FTE deployments for FY 2000 were unavailable and were assumed to be equal to FTE deployments for FY 2001, because both years were pre-GWOT, which began in late FY 2001. Surgeons, of course, do not spend all their time performing inpatient procedures. Preoperative and postoperative time would be recorded in MEPRS as a B code for the appropriate clinic.

Effects of Converting Inpatient Facilities to Stand-Alone Clinics

Another contributing factor in the decline of AFMS workload has been the conversion of many inpatient hospitals to stand-alone clinics, which means they no longer perform inpatient procedures. Chapter Two discussed the reduction in MTFs and the conversion of some inpatient MTFs to stand-alone clinics. In particular, from FY 2000 to FY 2007, eight inpatient facilities were converted to stand-alone clinics;[14] two additional inpatient MTFs were converted to ASCs in FY 2008 and FY 2009 (Air Force Academy and Andrews AFB hospitals). By FY 2007, about 7,000 RWPs annually had been lost because of these conversions, based on the workload performed at these same facilities in FY 2000. The forecast loss after completion of the Air Force Academy and Andrews AFB MTF conversions in FY 2009 is a total of 10,000 RWPs annually. Assuming these facilities do not regain inpatient capabilities, AFMS has permanently lost these RWPs.[15] Reflecting the overall trend of converting smaller hospitals to stand-alone clinics, the ten converted MTFs averaged less than 1,000 RWPs each in FY 2000, and excluding Andrews AFB, the average was less than 700 RWPs annually.

Effects of TRICARE for Life

Another factor contributing to the AFMS workload loss was passage of the TFL benefit in the FY 2001 National Defense Authorization Act, particularly because of its effect on the over-65 patient population. This population accounted for about 28 percent of the AFMS inpatient workload in FY 2007. Since TFL was implemented, all three services have lost workloads in the over-65 group, with AFMS losing the most. The Air Force had about 5,000 fewer RWPs in FY 2007 than in FY 2000. To avoid double counting, we excluded the over-65 workload from hospitals that had closed or were converted to outpatient MTFs. This calculation left us with the over-65 workload lost at hospitals still operating as inpatient facilities in FY 2007. The RWP trends are shown in Figure 5.6. In addition to the losses during this period, many in MHS are concerned that this population, once it has transitioned to civilian health-care providers, will see little benefit in obtaining care from an MTF even after MTF capabilities are restored, such as after GWOT deployments are reduced or eliminated.

Certainly, it is difficult to prove a cause-and-effect relationship between TFL and lost workload in the over-65 population. Some of the workload could have been lost for other reasons, such as the unavailability of deployed providers. Because the over-65 population has a lower priority at the MTF than the active-duty members and their dependents, the lower MTF capacity may have forced the older population to seek care under TFL from civilian medical care providers, especially for nonelective surgery. But the provisions of TFL also make purchased care more attractive because they eliminate the patient's out-of-pocket costs (the costs in excess of the Medicare reimbursement). Military retirees qualifying for Medicare must pay

---

[14] These were the hospitals at Grand Forks AFB, Sheppard AFB, Shaw AFB, Luke AFB, Incirlik AB (Turkey), Offutt AFB, MacDill AFB, and Spangdahlem AB (Germany).

[15] Unless there is a policy of transporting patients from the closed facilities to other AFMS inpatient facilities, the workload would go to purchased care or to another service's MTF. Patients at the two overseas facilities (Incirlik and Spangdahlem) would likely be transported to another MHS facility rather than be sent to a local, non-U.S. health-care facility.

Figure 5.6
Over-65 Relative Weighted Products, by Service, Excluding Closed Hospitals

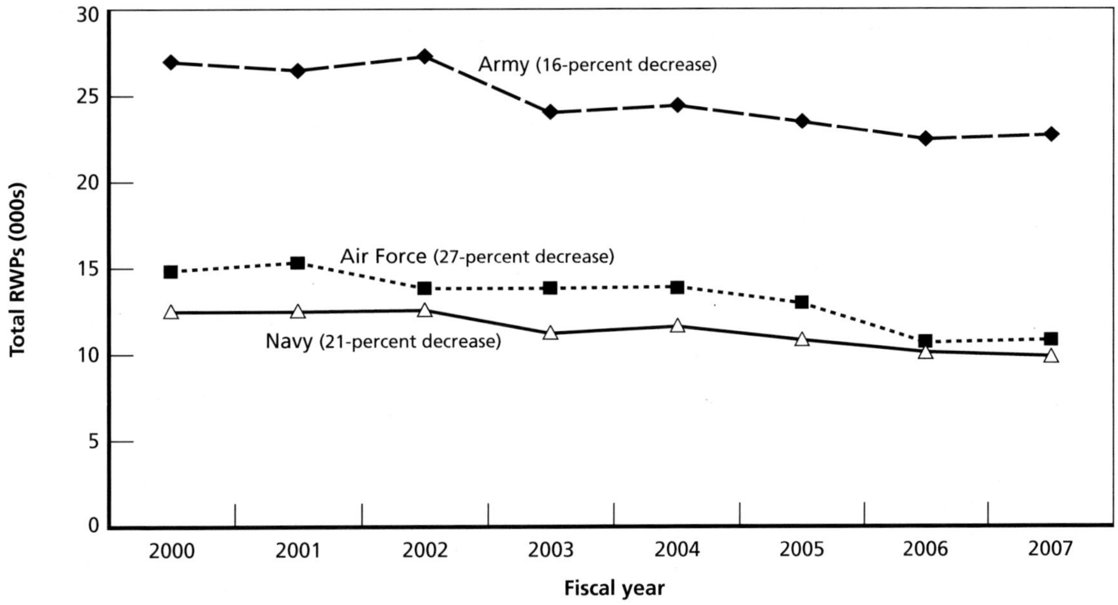

SOURCE: Data extracted by AFMOA for RAND.
RAND *TR859-5.6*

only the Medicare Part B monthly charge, currently just under $100 per month per covered individual.[16]

The outpatient workload for retirees over age 65 has also declined since FY 2000. In AFMS, however, this population received only about 7 percent of all outpatient procedures (RVUs) performed in FY 2007, considerably less than the share of inpatient workload (28 percent). Figure 5.7 shows the trends in outpatient workloads for the services.[17]

Again, AFMS lost the highest percentage, but workloads in all three services declined similarly. These losses are not as financially significant as losses of inpatient workload because the earnings per RVU are about 1/150th of an RWP on average and because the training and currency of critical-care specialists are not derived directly from providing outpatient care. Still, reductions in outpatient care could affect inpatient care because most inpatient care originates with an outpatient or emergency room visit. Thus, an institution that has only outpatient care may not be as attractive to this population. Some beneficiaries might select a civilian internist or multispecialty group practice over a smaller MTF for outpatient care because such an environment might provide access to specialists with the appropriate clinical training for the complex cases typically seen in the senior population.

---

[16] This premium is based on an income of less than about $85,000 for an individual or $170,000 for a married couple. The premium increases with income.

[17] We obtained outpatient workload trend data for the three services for FYs 2000 through 2007 and removed workload for any MTFs that had closed during the period. However, no adjustments were made for MTFs that converted from hospitals to stand-alone clinics, since much of that workload could continue to be performed in an outpatient facility.

Figure 5.7
Over-65 Relative Value Units, by Service, Excluding Closed Hospitals

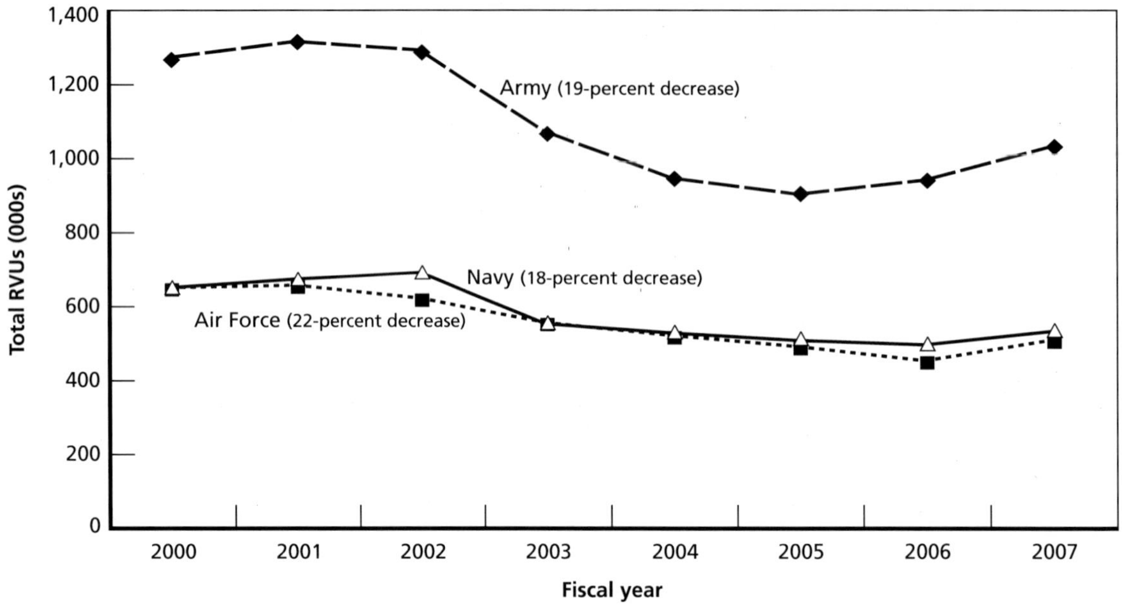

SOURCE: Data extracted by AFMOA for RAND.
RAND *TR859-5.7*

Keesler AFB Hospital and Hurricane Katrina

In September 2005, Hurricane Katrina struck Louisiana and Mississippi and severely damaged the AFMS hospital at Keesler AFB.[18] The consequences were dramatic: It took about a year for the hospital to start functioning again. All inpatient work stopped during FY 2006, and ambulatory work decreased considerably. Inpatient work resumed in FY 2007, but resulted in only a little more than 1,000 RWPs, where there had been more than 7,000 in FY 2000 (see Figure 5.8).[19]

Replacements for Deployed Medical Personnel

One final subject related to the effects of deployments on workload is the use of replacement personnel, often referred to as *backfills*. As medical personnel deploy, the military services have some limited opportunities to obtain replacements from the National Guard, reserves, other MTFs,[20] or through outside contracted civilian medical staff. Despite some obvious inefficiencies during the transition of replacements, such as getting schedules to mesh, some initial

---

[18] During the 2005 BRAC process, the Secretary of Defense initially recommended converting Keesler into an ASC. Later, however, the commission itself recommended to the President that the Keesler medical center instead be converted into a community hospital. See also Chapter Two.

[19] Medical personnel from Keesler might have been assigned elsewhere (either permanently or temporarily) while the hospital was out of commission and could have been performing its workload at other MTFs, but the closure and reopening certainly would have resulted in reduced efficiency by these personnel during the transition.

[20] Deploying medical personnel from one location to another would not necessarily change the overall AFMS workload unless deployed medical personnel were underemployed at their home bases.

Figure 5.8
Workload at Keesler Air Force Base, FYs 2000–2007

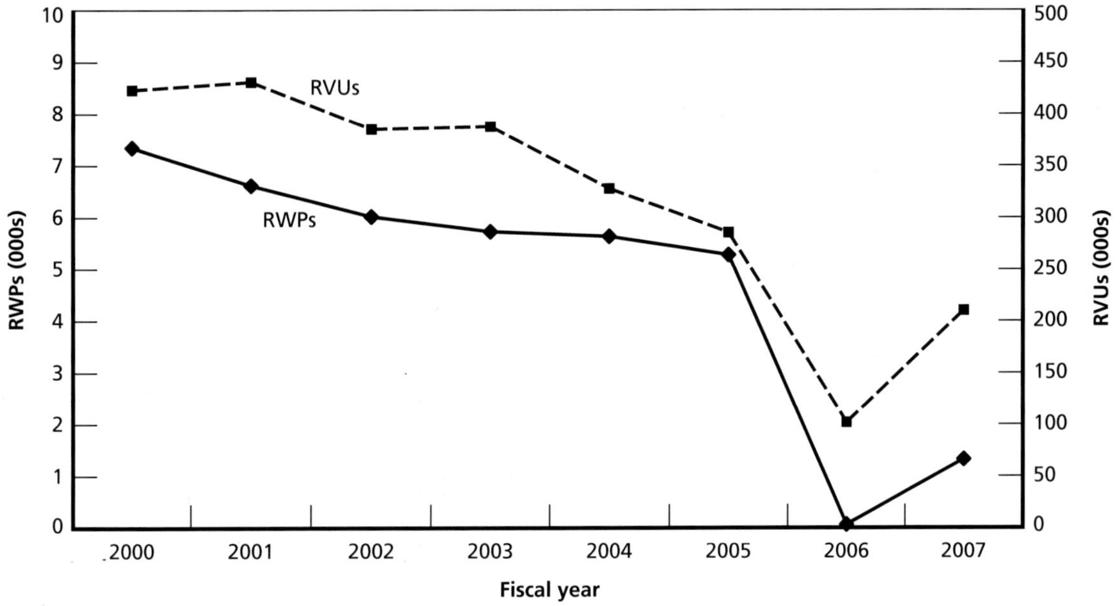

SOURCE: Data extracted by AFMOA for RAND.
RAND *TR859-5.8*

familiarization with procedures at an MTF, and delays in the contracting process, it would seem that finding replacements for deployed personnel could alleviate at least some of the lost workload.

We were unable to obtain data on the number of Air Force Reserve or Air National Guard personnel working in AFMS MTFs to replace deployed active-duty medical personnel. However, our interviews with Air National Guard personnel indicated that backfills of critical-care specialists at CONUS MTFs were negligible. Air National Guard personnel who were called or volunteered for active duty preferred to deploy to in-theater hospitals rather than backfill at CONUS MTFs. We did obtain data on contracts let for surgeons (45XX AFSCs) and emergency room physicians (44EX AFSC). AFMS turned to contract civilian physicians to backfill only about 16 percent of the deployed surgeons and emergency room physicians in FY 2007. Indeed, in FY 2007 a total of only 12 FTEs were contracted out in the entire AFMS.[21] AFMS personnel reported little success in contracting for physicians, in contrast to Army medical personnel, who reported having success in finding contract backfills. Several reasons were offered for this difference: many AFMS MTFs are in more remote areas where contract surgeons and emergency room physicians could not be found; the Army was more aggressive in contracting; or the differences in the length of Army and Air Force deployments made the longer Army contracts more appealing. The Army's policy has been to send its medical personnel to Southwest Asia for longer tours, usually one year. Until FY 2008, the Air Force generally had shorter

---

[21] The calculated 16 percent assumes surgeons and emergency room physicians are contracted to backfill for deployments only. According to AFMS deployment data, approximately 19 emergency room physicians and 57 surgeon FTEs were deployed in FY 2007; 12 divided by 76 yields 15.8 percent.

tours (four to six months).[22] Shorter contracts are less likely to appeal to a civilian surgeon or emergency room physician, who might have to give up a civilian practice or another job. One solution for AFMS might be to contract backfills for longer periods and have the contracted physician fill in for successively deployed physicians at the same MTF.

AFMS has been much more successful in contracting for nurses. It had a total of 212 nurse FTEs on contract in FY 2007, while 187 nurse FTEs were deployed. Although it was not within the scope of our project to determine which were backfills and which were contracted for normal peacetime augmentation of active-duty nurses, the large number of nurses contracted relative to the number deployed indicates that it is easier to attract and contract for nurses.

Summary

All aspects of the AFMS workload have decreased significantly since FY 2000, much more so than the Army's workload and somewhat greater than the Navy's. The inpatient workload decreased by over 23,000 admissions; there were 3 million fewer outpatient visits; and 2 million fewer prescriptions were filled.

These decreases have consequences not only for the distribution of funding under OSD workload-based methodologies but also in decreased opportunities for training and maintaining the currency and readiness of AFMS medical personnel, especially critical-care specialists. We examined the potential causes of the decrease, first in terms of readiness activities that negatively affect home-station workloads (but which are difficult to quantify).

We also addressed several factors that contributed to the 23,000-RWP decrease between FY 2000 and FY 2007: more growth than in the Army or Navy in the number of readiness FTEs, especially a 400-percent increase in the number of deployed surgeons; a loss of about 7,000 RWPs because of the conversion of hospitals to stand-alone clinics or ASCs; a loss of about 5,500 RWPs among the over-65 population; and a loss of about 6,000 RWPs because of hurricane damage at Keesler AFB.

In Chapter Six, we will discuss options for AFMS to try to recapture some of the lost workload.

---

[22] Adding two to three months of preparation and reconstitution to both Army and Air Force deployments provides a better estimate of the total time spent away from the home MTF.

Options Available for Recapturing and Expanding Workloads

If its decreasing workload trends continue unabated, AFMS may face an inpatient workload crisis in the coming years. Continued decreases would mean further reductions in PPS and MERHCF earnings,[1] would jeopardize training and maintaining the currency of critical-care specialists, could complicate recruiting and retention of critical-care specialists (if they perceive that AFMS inpatient opportunities are limiting their competency and professional progression), and could make it more and more difficult to continue operating the remaining nine CONUS hospitals in a post-GWOT environment.[2] This chapter outlines four options available to AFMS to recapture and/or increase AFMS critical-care specialists' inpatient workloads:

- expand opportunities at existing AFMS facilities
- assign Air Force providers to shared or joint hospitals
- increase cooperation with nonmilitary hospitals
- increase reliance on the Air National Guard and Air Force Reserve during wartime.

This chapter will discuss each of these options in detail. They are not all-inclusive and could be considered individually or in combination, depending on the situation at each MTF and the population in its catchment area. Although this chapter discusses some of the issues pertaining to each option, a full assessment of each option should be conducted before it is implemented.

One option (increasing workload at the AFMS MTFs) has the potential to address all four issues: funding, currency, professional opportunities, and retention of hospitals as training platforms. The others could provide opportunities for training and maintaining the currency of critical-care specialists but would not necessarily solve the other three issues.

In the current GWOT environment, with adequate supplemental funding each year to support military operations, financial resources do not appear to be a binding constraint on AFMS's ability to carry out its mission, based on our interviews with a wide range of experts. The proposed and actual reductions in funding due to PPS and other initiatives over the last few years represent a small share of total AFMS resources, although they produce an inordinate effect when taken from the more flexible O&M appropriation during the budget execution year. As discussed in Chapter Four, AFMS efforts to improve the accuracy and timeliness of

---

[1] A declining workload could reduce costs, but the magnitude of the reduction would depend on the nature of the cost components. For example, fixed costs, operating costs, and personnel costs would change at different rates.

[2] Maintenance of a hospital force structure entails consideration of the costs versus the potential earnings of each but also affects the development of senior leadership for AFMS. Commanding a hospital provides unique and significant training to officers being groomed for more senior positions in the AFMS and joint environments.

record-keeping (thereby improving workload metrics) and administrative actions, such as closing SADR cases promptly, could attenuate these reductions somewhat.

Maintaining Clinical Currency of Providers

For AFMS, maintaining provider clinical currency, especially its critical-care specialists and consequently its ability to fulfill its wartime mission, appears to be a more pressing concern than budget distributions.[3] With the GWOT, the Air Force has been called on to support full combat-support hospitals that serve not only deployed Air Force personnel but also personnel from the other military services. Indeed, the Air Force now plays a major role in operating Level III theater hospitals at Balad AB in Iraq, Bagram AB in Afghanistan, and in Qatar. In addition, the Air Force supplies significant manpower to the Army's Landstuhl Regional Medical Center (LRMC) in Germany, with Air Force medical personnel performing about 20 percent of its inpatient and ambulatory workloads. Providing wartime medical support for large numbers of ground forces changes not only the population at risk but the nature of the expected injuries that AFMS personnel must have the training and currency to treat. The requirements for supporting these major undertakings have tasked some AFMS specialists at higher rates than expected for AEF requirements.

If AFMS's current support to the GWOT permanently changes doctrine for DoD medical planning, it would force the Air Force to maintain responsibility for this type and scope of wartime mission. However, current AFMS requirements and opportunities may be insufficient in the context of the peacetime patient population and workload available at AFMS MTFs.

Previous studies, although somewhat dated, suggest that there is limited overlap between the peacetime duties performed at DoD MTFs and the battlefield injuries and disease and nonbattlefield injuries encountered during wartime. Hosek, Buchanan, and Goldberg (1985) suggests that family and general practitioners, internists, and pediatricians could carry out basic resuscitation and minor surgical procedures with some training, but they are not sufficiently prepared to undertake more-complicated procedures. Emergency medicine physicians can perform a broad range of tasks, but there are few places in AFMS where these personnel can keep current during peacetime. Moreover, the only major trauma center in AFMS, currently located at WHMC, will soon move to BAMC as part of the integration of these two centers.

A second relevant study compared diagnoses treated in peacetime with those expected in wartime using data from Vietnam (CBO, 1995). The authors found some overlap between peacetime MTF care and disease and nonbattlefield injuries, although the most common wartime diseases and nonbattlefield injuries did not appear in peacetime MTFs. There also was little overlap between peacetime MTF work and injuries among those wounded in action. During deployments, physicians are most likely to treat patients for wounds, fractures, and fevers, while peacetime care is dominated by obstetric care and conditions associated with aging.

---

[3]   AFMS commissioned RAND to do a follow-on study to evaluate this option further during FY 2010.

To support these missions, the Air Force might consider several options to expand opportunities to promote readiness among its medical personnel.[4] The Air Force could consider not only opportunities within the Air Force, the broader MHS, and the federal health system but also opportunities at civilian emergency rooms and trauma centers.

Option 1: Expand Opportunities at Existing Air Force Medical Service Facilities

The Air Force's first option is to expand readiness opportunities within AFMS. This option is clearly preferable to the others because increasing the workload would increase funding, provide additional opportunities for currency, enhance the image of AFMS, and justify the retention or expansion of the current hospital structure. However, older studies raised have observed that the peacetime Air Force caseload did not provide the trauma workload required to maintain readiness (Hosek, Buchanan, and Goldberg, 1985; CBO, 1995). Moreover, as discussed in Chapter Two, the Air Force has, since the time of those earlier studies, closed or reclassified many of its hospitals to stand-alone clinics, with primary care as the main workload. These changes reinforce earlier concerns about insufficient opportunities to maintain the type of currency necessary for AFMS critical-care readiness, especially in light of AFMS's expanded responsibilities during the GWOT. As noted earlier, peacetime surgery is not comparable to wartime trauma surgery, but it is the best substitute outside a trauma center for critical-care specialists.

AFMS focus on primary care clinics may not, however, be inappropriate. First, Air Force beneficiaries consist of a relatively young and healthy active-duty population and their families, who require advanced care less frequently than the U.S. population in general. Second, TFL has decreased financial liabilities for the over-65 population, who might require more advanced health care but who are also alleviated of the burden to pay for purchased care under TFL. Consequently, not all AFMS sites need to staff a large range of specialties for primary care. Indeed, it may be difficult to justify certain specialties at some remote AFMS MTFs because the demand may not be great enough to ensure quality of care (i.e., enough workload to keep specialists current).

One option is to maintain the current stand-alone primary care clinics but supplement them with a handful of larger MTFs that offer a substantial spectrum of specialties. These larger MTFs should be chosen because of their ability to generate sufficient demand from the eligible beneficiary population to sustain currency. These larger MTFs also should maintain graduate medical education (GME) programs or ties to local GME programs, which are necessary both to attract and to keep medical professionals and students current. This approach could be called the "high-low mix," with the majority of primary care stand-alone clinics offering limited specialty care, and a smaller number of hospitals and ASCs offering a wider range of specialties. This is much like the current AFMS strategy.

---

[4] In this context, readiness consists of military medical personnel seeing the appropriate medical cases (in terms of number and severity) to allow providers, especially in critical-care specialties, to maintain sufficient currency to deploy within the time specified in the deployment plan and successfully perform their wartime mission of providing health care to deployed personnel and other populations, as required.

Of course, currency and GME accreditation depend largely on an adequate caseload. To support expansion of the larger MTFs, AFMS will need to recapture work that the civilian sector currently performs. This will be critical after GWOT deployments end or decrease significantly and as more critical-care specialists return to their home MTFs. The absence of the wartime workload will increase not only an MTF's capabilities to manage the inpatient workload but also the need for its specialists to keep current via the peacetime workload. The feasibility of such a plan would depend on the supply and demand for these specialties. Questions about the types of beneficiaries in an MTF's catchment area (e.g., retirees that are Medicare-eligible), the share of work performed in the civilian sector, and the type of care provided by the civilian sector become relevant.

Competition from other providers is also important for deciding which, if any, MTFs can support additional specialties. Many of the major Air Force MTFs are in areas with competing health-care infrastructures in the private and federal sector. Competition for MHS beneficiaries and complex cases may arise from VA hospitals, academic or teaching hospitals, and hospitals with Level I trauma centers.

For example, one possibility would be to establish a trauma center at an existing AFMS MTF. Official designation of a hospital as a trauma center is determined by a regional governmental authority. For a Level I Trauma Center to be considered "verified," the American College of Surgeons requires one of the following minimum patient volumes:

- 1,200 trauma patients per year
- 240 admissions with injury severity scores (ISSs) greater than 15
- an average of 35 patients with ISSs greater than 15 for trauma surgeons.[5]

In addition to these minimum requirements, trauma centers must maintain a variety of specialties, such as neurosurgery and orthopedics. In essence, there would need to be a requirement for a tertiary care facility with sufficient patient volume to maintain the currency of trauma specialties.

As Table 6.1 shows, most major AFMS MTFs are in areas that already have trauma centers. In a few cases, the nearest trauma center is more than 20 miles away. Of course, the presence or absence of a trauma center near the MTF is not sufficient to determine whether a new trauma center should be built: Areas with larger populations can justify multiple trauma centers, while areas with smaller populations may not provide enough workload to maintain certification for even one trauma center.

Determining the ability to generate a sufficient caseload for currency and accreditation requires an analysis of the potential demand and existing supply of these services. Data sources on proxies for demand among the general population are available from the Healthcare Cost and Utilization Project and include data on utilization of emergency rooms and hospitals.[6]

---

[5] The ISS system is a means of assessing a patient with multiple injuries by using an overall score. Each injury is assigned an Abbreviated Injury Scale score and is located in one of six body regions—head, face, chest, abdomen, extremities (including pelvis), and external. Only the highest Abbreviated Injury Scale score in each body region is counted for the next step. The scores for the three most severely injured body regions are squared and summed to produce the ISS score. (See Brohi, 2007.)

[6] The Healthcare Cost and Utilization Project is a family of health-care databases and related software tools and products developed through a federal-state-industry partnership and sponsored by the Agency for Healthcare Research and Quality. Through its website, the project brings together the data-collection efforts of states, hospital associations, private organizations, and the federal government to create a national information resource for patient-level health-care data.

Table 6.1
Selected AFMS MTFs and Nearby Trauma Centers

Installation	City	Trauma Center	Distance (mi)	Level[a]
Air Force Academy	Colorado Springs	Penrose–St. Francis	11	II
		Memorial	19	II
Andrews AFB	Washington, D.C.	Howard University	12	I
		George Washington University (among others)	13	I
Davis-Monthan AFB	Tucson	University Medical Center	6	I
Eglin AFB	Pensacola	Baptist	49	II
		Sacred Heart	50	II
Elmendorf AFB	Anchorage	Alaska Native Medical Center	6	II
Keesler AFB	Pascagoula	Singing River	25	II
Lackland AFB	San Antonio	Brooke Army	17	I
		University	12	I
Langley AFB	Newport News	Riverside Regional	6	II
	Norfolk	Sentara Norfolk General	19	I
Luke AFB	Phoenix	St. Joseph's	22	I
		John C. Lincoln	22	I
MacDill AFB	Tampa	Tampa General	8	I
Mountain Home AFB	Boise	St. Alphonsus	57	II
Nellis AFB	Las Vegas	University Medical Center of Southern Nevada	10	I
Offutt AFB	Omaha	Creighton University	12	I
		University of Nebraska	12	I
Scott AFB	St. Louis	St. Louis University	27	I
		Barnes-Jewish	26	I
Travis AFB	Sacramento	University of California, Davis	42	I
Wright-Patterson AFB	Dayton	Miami Valley	10	I

[a] The level listed indicates that of the associated civilian trauma center.

These data allow an analysis of the relevant caseload by diagnosis for each hospital or area for participating states. Data on the availability of health infrastructure and personnel—including identified shortages and underserved areas—are available by county in hospital and area resource file data sets.

An area that is more difficult to assess using data is AFMS's ability to recapture the workload of beneficiaries who currently use purchased care, especially those eligible for TFL.[7] Using the AFMS guidelines for general surgeons, justifying an additional surgical specialty or surgeon requires an increase of more than 15,000 in the enrolled population, so recapturing or enrolling enough of the population to provide sufficient workload for surgical currency would be a large undertaking at an MTF.

---

[7] The additional workload from TFL-eligible patients could benefit AFMS clinically but would increase expenses by incurring the full cost of providing care at an MTF. Under purchased care, DoD pays only the amount Medicare does not pay. Hence, a strong case would have to be made for the currency requirement to bring the Medicare-eligible patient population back to the MTFs.

One consideration in examining opportunities to increase workload is the characteristics of the current AFMS MTF inpatient population. In FY 2007, the 38,400 inpatient admissions were almost evenly divided among four groups:

- active-duty personnel, 24 percent
- dependents of active-duty personnel, 25 percent
- retirees, 25 percent
- dependents of retirees and others, 26 percent.

Unlike the Army, whose force structure has grown by more than 10 percent since FY 2000 because of the GWOT, the Air Force active-duty population has decreased by about 7 percent and is expected to stabilize around 330,000 for the foreseeable future. Thus, there will likely be few opportunities to expand the active-duty workload at AFMS MTFs. Presumably the same is true for their dependents, assuming that the ratios of marriage and family sizes stay about the same. Thus, growth in patient workload will have to come from retirees and their families.

Option 2: Assign Air Force Providers to Shared or Joint Hospitals

An alternative to expanding opportunities in AFMS MTFs would be to leverage opportunities across the entire MHS by assigning AFMS specialists to Army or Navy MTFs. Such assignments could enhance the currency of AFMS personnel, providing a wider range of experiences for those participating in the program, matching available staff with MTFs that have larger workloads, recapturing workload from purchased care, and maintaining AFMS personnel in a military culture. The process might need to be more structured, however, to ensure long-term opportunities for AFMS providers. One concern with this option is that such opportunities may be limited; both the CBO and Hosek studies indicated a shortage in opportunities to provide specialized care across all services.

Another major consideration would be to determine how to attribute earnings to the parent service for specialists assigned to other services' MTFs. The service receiving the additional providers would see workload increases at its MTFs and, therefore, an earnings increase under PPS and MERHCF but would not bear the initial training, salaries, and other personnel costs of the "loaned" specialists. Conversely, the parent service would lose the workload produced when its specialists are assigned to another service.

There are, however, several examples of emerging collaborations among the services in key markets, particularly in San Antonio and the National Capital Region, which may provide useful prototypes. AFMS is partnered with the Army Medical Department in the development of SAMMC, which is an integration of AFMS's WHMC and BAMC. The proposed result is a single entity, SAMMC, with two campuses: SAMMC South (formerly WHMC) and SAMMC North (formerly BAMC). Specialties will be spread across the two campuses, and assignment of Army and Air Force staff to the campuses will depend on their clinical specialties rather than on their service affiliations. Currently, leadership positions are joint, such that the best-qualified individuals from either service are selected as department chairs. Executive leadership for administrative purposes, however, has not been determined. If successful, this effort could be considered a model for additional collaborations among the services.

The current plan is for the Air Force to fund all AFMS military personnel costs in SAMMC, as well as the civilian personnel and operating costs of the SAMMC South facility. The Army will fund all Army military personnel costs and the civilian personnel and operating costs of the SAMMC North facility. However, with all the inpatient workload transitioning to SAMMC North, the Army stands to gain significant earnings credit, while AFMS stands to lose all inpatient earnings if the current workload identification and funding under PPS and MERHCF are sustained.[8]

DoD is working on several initiatives that could facilitate proper record-keeping, which would help enable interservice sharing of medical personnel. These initiatives include NPI and DMHRSi. These systems would allow AFMS to track the labor hours AFMS providers spend in partner facilities and the workload of AFMS providers there. This would allow AFMS to claim at least its providers' inpatient workload as part of its PPS or MERHCF earnings, regardless of whether the inpatient facilities were considered part of AFMS.

The senior military officials we interviewed considered assigning AFMS providers to other military services' MTFs to maintain their currency desirable because such assignments provide opportunities for providers to keep current while remaining immersed in the military culture. But, as stated previously, it may not be feasible to accommodate all AFMS specialist personnel in other services' MTFs if the workload in their specialties is insufficient. DoD beneficiaries may not represent the full spectrum of cases or provide enough of the caseload required for clinical currency.

Option 3: Increase Cooperation with Nonmilitary Hospitals

Another opportunity for AFMS to increase its workload may be increased cooperation with nonmilitary hospitals. CBO (1995) and U.S. General Accounting Office (1998) indicate that civilian trauma centers offer opportunities for the appropriate caseload for clinical currency.

If AFMS cannot find sufficient opportunities in DoD facilities for its personnel to maintain currency, particularly in the critical-care and surgical skill areas, assigning them to other federal facilities would be in the best interests of the government. Using military personnel, particularly clinical staff and medical or surgical specialists, could help reduce the direct costs of providing care that the federal government must otherwise pay for directly. The best opportunities would be to affiliate with the VA and the Indian Health Service. Other opportunities might include the Bureau of Prisons and the Department of Health and Human Services in support of Health Resources and Services Administration–funded community clinics, as well as direct support to federally funded public-private partnership humanitarian missions. Although not providing the same workload mix as a civilian trauma center, the veteran population would be older and could offer a representative mix of workload to help retain currency.

Establishing partnerships with the VA and its VHA makes sense for a number of reasons. Cooperation between DoD and the VA is increasing, with increasing emphasis on partnering, sharing medical information, and supporting seamless patient transitions. Assigning DoD staff to VA facilities would promote seamless transitions and inculcate a spirit of cooperation and understanding between the two departments. The VA has a large eligible population of

---

[8] However, RVU earnings could be higher at SAMMC South if the ambulatory surgery workload increased under the consolidation. Appendix E discusses this overall issue in more detail.

older veterans with many serious health conditions. It operates the largest health-care system in the United States, with approximately 175 hospitals divided into 21 Veterans Integrated Service Networks. Many of the VA's major medical centers are close to military bases, which could provide administrative support to AFMS personnel. More than 8 million veterans are enrolled for care, and approximately 25 million are eligible for care; more than 70 percent have chronic health problems. Approximately 50 percent are over 65. The VA directly funds almost 10 percent of all medical residents in the United States and has academic affiliations with over 100 medical schools. The VA also has critical shortages of nurses in many areas and could use loaned AFMS staff.

Assigning AFMS staff to VA facilities would offer AFMS some important advantages. Staff could be assigned to large teaching facilities. Clinicians could receive academic appointments. Because the VA is a federal organization, state licensure and liability insurance would not be issues. VA hospitals could also use certain enlisted personnel, such as respiratory therapists and other specialists. Other enlisted specialties would require greater coordination, but arrangements could be worked out if both the military and the VA were interested. The beneficiary population provides opportunities for significant surgical workloads in orthopedics, general surgery, and cardiothoracic surgery that could, for example, fully utilize surgical teams and critical-care unit specialists. Most importantly, serving the veteran population would likely be perceived as worthwhile because of common values and experiences that active-duty military personnel and veterans share.

A successful DoD-VA partnership would require a long-term commitment and perhaps an AFMS commitment to overstaffing so as to not completely halt specialty care if staff were deployed. It also would require sensitivity to the preexisting academic affiliations of some of the adjunct VA staff.

The Indian Health Service also operates federally funded hospitals, the three largest being in Phoenix, Arizona; Gallup, New Mexico; and Anchorage, Alaska. Typically, these hospitals have academic affiliations with the VA and use electronic health records very similar to those of the VA. The Bureau of Prisons provides another opportunity, as do Department of Health and Human Services–funded community health centers, which are often staffed with commissioned officers of the Public Health Service. The Air Force has an international health specialist program that could be used to leverage AFMS clinical skills and provide opportunities to deliver specialized care in humanitarian missions on a semipermanent basis.

Another option for external partnerships would be with nonfederal civilian hospitals. DoD currently has two main types of relationships with civilian hospitals. First, DoD operates such programs as the Center for the Sustainment of Trauma and Readiness Skills, under which military medical personnel are temporarily assigned to work in civilian trauma centers to "tune" their skills just before a deployment. This program provides valuable just-in-time training in treating trauma cases, but providers typically spend a month or less at a hospital. Longer-term assignments are rare.

Second, some MTFs have established longer-term partnerships with local hospitals. Under these partnerships, providers assigned to an MTF can use the inpatient facilities of the civilian hospital to serve DoD beneficiary patients. These providers have longer-term relationships with local hospitals, but generally spend only the time required for the inpatient procedures and follow-up visits there. Preoperative and postoperative visits normally take place at the MTF. Although these inpatient procedures provide practice for surgeons and reduce the cost of purchased care, TMA must still reimburse the hospital for its share of the costs (facility and support staff costs). Moreover, while the patients are DoD beneficiaries requiring inpatient care, they are typically not trauma cases. In FY 2008, AFMS had external partnerships at six civilian hospitals and earned $539,000 in reimbursements for the work performed at the facilities. The six facilities were Tampa General Hospital, Tampa Bay Surgical Center, and Fort Walton Beach Medical Center, all in Florida; Del Webb Memorial Hospital and Banner Estrella Medical Center, both in Arizona; and Nix Medical Center in Texas.

One potential opportunity for AFMS to increase the currency of its specialists may be to create external assignments for AFMS providers to work full time at external facilities, particularly trauma centers, providing care to patients there regardless of the patient's DoD beneficiary status.

Table 6.2 shows the key differences between existing external partnerships and these proposed external assignments.

Such opportunities exist, but a key issue is the willingness of civilian and federal hospitals to accept assignments from the services. One survey examined opportunities for external assignments and found that civilian hospitals would be willing to take on military medical personnel and, potentially, contribute to their labor costs (Eibner, 2008). There was particular support for the use of military personnel to provide short-term acute care. Suitable specialties could include surgeons, anesthesiologists, urologists, dermatologists, radiologists, cardiologists, orthopedists, nurses, and some technicians.

Interestingly, the study found that the possible deployment of military personnel was not considered a barrier to accepting them. However, the respondents indicated that deployment might affect how military personnel were used in the hospital. One option would be to assign military personnel to elective surgery only because it could be planned in advance. However, this would reduce the usefulness of the assignment for DoD, at least for some critical-care specialties. Alternatively, the military could stagger deployments and provide overstaffing in a 5:4 ratio (e.g., five personnel assigned to an MTF for every four authorizations) to reduce the disruption deployments would cause. Eibner (2008) also provides a thorough assessment of the advantages and disadvantages of external partnerships for DoD.

Hospitals that have staff shortages or an acute need for the specialties AFMS offers may be more willing to accept military personnel. As noted previously, hospitals in remote locations,

Table 6.2
Key Differences Between External Partnerships and External Assignments

Issue	External Partnership	External Assignment
Air Force provider is assigned to . . .	Air Force MTF	External hospital
Patients seen by an Air Force provider include . . .	Any enrolled DoD beneficiaries (most likely at local MTF)	Any patient
The Air Force provider spends time at external hospital . . .	As needed to perform inpatient procedures and immediate follow-up visits	Full-time
Cost recovery is based on . . .	Professional component of cost credited to MTF; institutional portion paid to hospital by TRICARE	No workload credit or payment to MTF; service absorbs personnel costs of provider as a cost of maintaining readiness. (Some cost recovery may be possible.)

safety-net hospitals, and those serving other federal populations (e.g., Indian Health Service) could be considered.

From the Air Force's point of view, one potential concern about external assignments is that the absence of a military culture may reduce the medical personnel's connection to the Air Force. A recent RAND study shows that Air Force physicians who serve their residencies in civilian hospitals do not stay in the Air Force as long as those who serve their residencies in military hospitals (Keating et al., 2009). This finding raises concerns that Air Force physicians who are assigned to civilian hospitals may also be less likely to stay in the Air Force. However, it may not be cultural differences that cause shorter careers but that specialties that are more likely to require civilian hospital residencies may also be those that pay more in the private sector. Also, medical personnel who are more likely to be oriented toward a military career may choose a military residency over a civilian one. Moreover, CBO (1995) points out that military specialists who train in civilian residency programs may leave the service sooner than those who train in military GME programs because of the way their service obligations are structured: Those who serve civilian residencies have typically not been sponsored through medical school by the military and therefore do not incur the same service obligation. This finding suggests that military personnel who spend time in civilian hospitals would not necessarily leave the Air Force sooner than if they had served in military hospitals.

Option 4: Increase Reliance on the Air National Guard and Reserves During Wartime

Other nations have relied primarily on reservists for deployments of medical personnel. Britain and Israel are two prominent examples. However, a key difference between these countries and the United States is that many physicians in Britain and Israel are employed in their national health-care systems, which can presumably accommodate the temporary loss of some physicians more easily because other personnel would be more readily available in the same system to maintain care for patients.

In contrast, most U.S. physicians are either partners or sole proprietors of medical practices. Many physicians must develop their own practices, so a potential disruption due to deployment is a more serious concern and generally bears an inverse relationship to the size of the practice. In larger partnerships, when physicians are called up for duty, the other partners may be able to take the additional caseload temporarily; if not, the patients will have to seek care elsewhere, as they would with a sole proprietorship. In a small practice, the disruption caused by a call-up could be a large burden on both the business and the patients.

Given the characteristics of the U.S. health-care system, our interviews suggest that the scope for the use of Air National Guard and Air Force Reserve personnel for AFMS deployments or even as backfill replacements for deploying physicians during wartime is limited. The primary concern from the point of view of medical personnel was the unpredictability of deployments or call-ups, the backfill requirements at civilian practices, and the duration of the required commitment (e.g., service days per three-year period). Moreover, in the Air National Guard, critical-care AFSCs have very low fill rates—ranging from 6 percent for general surgeons and anesthesiologists to 31 percent for operating room nurses.

In addition, reserve recruiting for critical-care specialists among medical school students or residents was seen to conflict with recruiting for active-duty medical requirements. A better solution may be to offer reserve affiliation bonuses for specialists completing their active-duty commitment but who might wish to serve in the Air National Guard or Air Force Reserve. However, the possibility of unanticipated deployments could still be an issue.

Summary

Given that Air Force active-duty end strengths are planned to stabilize near current levels, the only areas of likely inpatient growth are retirees and their dependents. Thus, it is imperative for AFMS leadership to consider nontraditional options for maintaining clinical currency. The options outlined in this chapter each have their own associated benefits and costs, and each requires further study and analysis to determine the most effective course of action.

None of these four options is likely to produce a robust critical-care specialist corps by itself, and even a combination of the four may not address all of AFMS's four key issues of critical-care specialist training and currency, professional competency, earnings, and retention of hospitals as training facilities. AFMS will have to assess each of the proposed options fully and pursue the most promising options persistently, given the time it takes to train surgeons and some of the other critical-care specialists.

CHAPTER SEVEN

Conclusions

The last two decades have been turbulent for AFMS, with significant reductions and other changes to its MTF structure; changes in wartime requirements from large, fixed, in-theater hospitals to a more streamlined EMEDS approach and, now, satisfying wartime taskings to operate three major hospitals in Afghanistan, Iraq, and Qatar; major reductions in inpatient, ambulatory, and prescription workloads; and the resulting implications for funding because of the implementation of OSD workload-oriented funding methodologies. So far, the effects of workload reductions on AFMS funding have been relatively minor, primarily because of ample wartime supplemental funding and savings found in other parts of its budget. During our interviews, no mention was made of AFMS not fulfilling its wartime tasking in support of the GWOT, and readiness activities reported in MEPRS confirm a high level of participation from AFMS personnel. Deploying critical-care specialists have been provided special predeployment currency training so that they have arrived in theater ready to perform successfully. Management of these specialties has been a challenge, based on our interviews, but one that has been met successfully so far.

However, as AFMS prepares to enter the second decade of the 21st century, major issues loom on the horizon. First is the decreasing workload, especially the inpatient workload. As of the end of FY 2007, inpatient workload had fallen 37 percent since FY 2000 for a variety of reasons addressed in previous chapters. This decline must be arrested because of

- the need to train and maintain the currency of critical-care specialists
- the need to maintain AFMS as a viable, vibrant medical organization that attracts and retains quality personnel
- the effects on AFMS earnings and budgets
- the need to maintain hospitals as training platforms and leadership opportunities for future AFMS senior officers and to demonstrate that AFMS is a robust, full-service health-care organization.

Increasing the workload will be a challenge, even after support to the GWOT deployments decreases and specialists can return to their MTFs full time. Enactment of the TFL benefit, which reduces the attractiveness of direct care for Medicare-eligible beneficiaries, will make drawing a larger share of this population back to MTFs difficult. Attracting the non–Medicare-eligible retirees and dependents who have been using purchased care because of a lack of care at MTFs during the GWOT may also be a challenge. In addition, AFMS workloads and capabilities must be built in a coordinated fashion, given the time needed to recruit and train some critical-care specialists. Increases in DoD health-care costs make it unlikely that OASD(HA) will abandon its "pay for performance" funding programs, so AFMS must restore its inpatient workload or find alternatives and get credit for them. However, given the earnings and expense ratios shown in Chapter Three, it is unlikely that MHS as a whole or AFMS in particular can be funded solely based on workloads; military-unique activities will still require funding that is not based on the workload.

We have identified four potential alternatives for AFMS to pursue, independently or (more advisably) in tandem, to enhance its critical-care capabilities:

- expand opportunities at existing AFMS facilities
- assign Air Force providers to shared or joint hospitals
- increase cooperation with nonmilitary hospitals, especially VHA hospitals
- increase reliance on the Air National Guard and Air Force Reserve during wartime.

We would suggest that future research focus on fleshing out these options and perhaps identifying new ones.[1]

AFMS also faces a doctrinal question about its role in future conflicts. Although it has fulfilled requirements to operate three in-theater hospitals, certain specialties, such as critical-care specialists and mental health professionals, have been in high demand. If this wartime role is expected to continue in future AFMS and DoD doctrine, the peacetime inpatient surgical workload will continue to be a vital aspect of keeping critical-care specialists trained and current. Defining and refining DoD's future expectations of AFMS would improve its ability to determine requirements for perhaps a larger cadre of wartime critical-care specialties and the amount of inpatient workload needed to keep them current.

In addition, AFMS must ensure that the work Air Force personnel perform is properly attributed to AFMS. This effort is critical because both funding and the perception of AFMS's contribution to DoD's health-care mission are, in some sense, associated with its workload. The merger of WHMC and BAMC into SAMMC is a good example of a larger transition taking place in MHS overall. The entire inpatient workload at SAMMC North will be the responsibility of both Air Force and Army personnel, but unless a new reporting process is established, the Army will get the credit and the associated funding for all of it. To ensure AFMS gets both resources and recognition for the workload it produces at SAMMC, we recommend that the AFMS leadership advocate with OASD(HA) for suspension of PPS and MERHCF funding methodologies until experience has demonstrated a fair allocation of resources and attribution of costs and workloads between the services.

More-accurate attribution of workloads is especially critical for the MILPERS appropriations. Some of the initiatives under way, such as DMHRSi and NPI, should help improve reporting and recognition of workloads throughout MHS and may allow clearer attribution of workloads to both providers and locations, thereby allowing allocation of earnings separately to providers and MTFs, where necessary. DMHRSi will provide information on the locations where military personnel work and solve the borrowed military manpower identification problem but will not necessarily properly allocate funding (especially the MILPERS funding) unless the rules for allocating earnings under PPS and MERHCF are modified.

Instead of relying on borrowed military manpower reporting in MEPRS, it may be more appropriate to propose a new performance measure, such as the FTEs one service contributes

---

[1]   The Air Force Surgeon General commissioned RAND to conduct such a study in FY 2010.

to another or to outside assignments, such as the VA. While these level-of-effort FTEs would not be an output metric (which would be preferred), they may be the best way to assess AFMS's contribution to mission accomplishment when AFMS staffing is significant. This change in personnel accounting would be important in three of the four alternatives discussed previously and could be used to justify staff and funding for MILPERS and indirect support costs, such as O&M funding for travel, training, and GME.

Another, lesser challenge, but one that is under AFMS's control, calls for AFMS management to enforce more-accurate reporting of providers' work hours in MEPRS. Reporting is a congressional requirement and unlikely to go away, but inaccurate reporting can reflect negatively on AFMS and can affect cost reporting and funding. Our interviewees almost universally told us that few medical personnel took accurate reporting seriously enough or understood the higher-level consequences of inaccurate reporting on service comparisons or funding. DMHRSi alone will not solve the problem of inaccurate reporting by individuals—personal discipline will still be required. While the MEPRS reporting system has significant limitations, we found nothing inherently wrong with it.[2]

Challenging times call for creative thinking, and it is highly unlikely that AFMS will be able to maintain optimum long-term viability using the same strategies it has employed in the past. Indeed, new realities will continue to drive new economics and require new strategies for AFMS to meet and maintain its many missions.

---

[2]   As noted earlier, guidance from the Surgeon General's office reinforces the need for accurate reporting using DMHRSi.

Medical Workload by Service Military Treatment Facility

Tables A.1, A.2, A.3, and A.4 show stepped-down MEPRS A and B costs by MTF, excluding prescription drug costs for the Air Force, Army, and Navy, arranged from the highest to lowest cost MTF. The tables also include earnings from PPS and MERHCF, excluding reimbursements for prescription costs. We treated prescription costs as pass-through expenses, since they do not reflect the level of care an MTF provides. The final column shows the share of expenses each MTF earns from PPS and MERHCF.

Table A.1
Comparison of Air Force FY 2007 MEPRS Stepped-Down A and B Expenses Against MERHCF and PPS Earnings, Top 30

Parent DMIS Identifier	Unit	Installation	Stepped-Down MEPRS A & B Expenses ($M)[a]	PPS and MERHCF Earnings ($M)[a]	Earnings Share (%)
Inpatient					
0117	59th MDW	Lackland AFB	399.2	357.0	89
0095	88th MDG	Wright Patterson AFB	121.0	109.6	91
0014	60th MDG	Travis AFB	135.2	143.0	106
0042	96th MDG	Eglin AFB	93.6	58.0	62
0066	79th MDG	Andrews AFB	81.2	49.4	61
0079	99th MDG	O'Callaghan Hospital	76.3	46.9	61
0120	1st MDG	Langley AFB	70.0	28.8	41
0073	81st MDG	Keesler AFB	62.6	38.4	61
0033	10th MDG	Air Force Academy	62.1	36.2	58
0006	3rd MDG	Elmendorf AFB	64.0	47.8	75
0053	366th MDG	Mountain Home AFB	21.2	9.4	44
Ambulatory					
0055	375th MDG	Scott AFB	34.8	15.1	43
0045	6th MDG	MacDill AFB	26.5	16.7	63
0078	55th MDG	Offutt AFB	33.6	16.4	49
0009	56th MDG	Luke AFB	23.3	12.9	55
0113	82nd MDG	Sheppard AFB	27.4	11.9	43
0043	325th MDG	Tyndall AFB	8.7	6.2	71
0083	377th MDG	Kirtland AFB	14.7	8.3	57
0252	21st MDG	Peterson AFB	12.7	8.8	69
0096	72nd MDG	Tinker AFB	14.7	10.3	71
0010	355th MDG	Davis Monthan AFB	13.2	10.1	77
0051	78th MDG	Robins AFB	15.1	7.0	46
0326	305th MDG	McGuire AFB	15.0	7.7	51
0119	75th MDG	Hill AFB	10.8	8.4	78
0366	12th MDG	Randolph AFB	13.5	8.3	62
0004	42nd MDG	Maxwell AFB	9.3	9.2	99
0112	7th MDG	Dyess AFB	11.0	5.1	47
0101	20th MDG	Shaw AFB	10.1	5.5	54
0062	2nd MDG	Barksdale AFB	8.8	6.2	70

[a] Excluding the costs of prescription ingredients.

Table A.2
Comparison of Air Force FY 2007 MEPRS Stepped-Down A and B Expenses Against MERHCF and PPS Earnings, Bottom 32

Parent DMIS Identifier	Unit	Installation	Stepped-Down MEPRS A & B Expenses ($M)[a]	PPS and MERHCF Earnings ($M)[a]	Earnings Share (%)
Ambulatory					
0128	92nd MDG	Fairchild AFB	10.7	5.9	56
0046	45th MDG	Patrick AFB	N/A[b]	8.4	N/A
7139	1st Special Ops MDG	Hurlburt AFB	12.9	6.4	49
0413	579th MDG	Bolling AFB	10.8	4.1	38
0090	4th MDG	Seymour Johnson AFB	9.1	5.4	59
0036	436th MDG	Dover AFB	10.5	6.6	63
0013	314th MDG	Little Rock AFB	11.1	5.7	52
0084	49th MDG	Holloman AFB	10.4	5.1	49
0287	15th MDG	Hickam AFB	10.9	4.6	43
0015	9th MDG	Beale AFB	9.0	3.9	43
0019	95th MDG	Edwards AFB	9.7	3.4	35
0395	62nd MDG	McChord AFB	8.7	4.6	53
0094	5th MDG	Minot AFB	9.7	4.0	41
0076	509th MDG	Whiteman AFB	9.5	4.2	45
0050	23rd MDG	Moody AFB	7.5	3.6	49
0335	43rd MDG	Pope AFB	10.3	3.7	36
7200	460th MDG	Buckley AFB	2.6	4.2	163
0106	28th MDG	Ellsworth AFB	8.7	3.9	45
0077	341st MDG	Malmstrom AFB	9.3	4.1	44
0018	30th MDG	Vandenberg AFB	8.4	3.7	45
0338	71st MDG	Vance AFB	4.4	1.9	44
0059	22nd MDG	McConnell AFB	6.5	4.9	75
0129	90th MDG	F.E. Warren AFB	7.4	3.2	44
0085	27th MDG	Cannon AFB	7.3	3.0	41
0310	66th MDG	Hanscom AFB	5.9	3.0	52
0356	437th MDG	Charleston AFB	6.9	4.4	64
0203	354th MDG	Eielson AFB	8.1	2.3	29
0093	319th MDG	Grand Forks AFB	7.5	2.4	33
0364	17th MDG	Goodfellow AFB	5.8	3.3	56
0074	14th MDG	Columbus AFB	5.9	3.0	52
0248	61st MDS	Los Angeles AFB	4.6	3.7	79
0097	97th MDG	Altus AFB	6.4	2.2	34
0114	47th MDG	Laughlin AFB	6.4	2.1	33

[a] Excluding the costs of prescription ingredients.

[b] We have chosen not to include stepped-down MEPRS A and B expenses excluding prescription costs for Patrick Air Force Base, as the data contained anomalies that could not be explained by AFMS.

Table A.3
Comparison of Army FY 2007 MEPRS Stepped-Down A and B Expenses Against MERHCF and PPS Earnings

Parent DMIS Identifier	Facility	Installation	Stepped-Down MEPRS A & B Expenses ($M)[a]	PPS and MERHCF Earnings ($M)[a]	Earnings Share (%)
Inpatient					
0037	Walter Reed AMC		386.7	368.3	95
0109	Brooke AMC		330.0	345.4	105
0052	Tripler AMC	Ft. Shafter	298.0	255.8	86
0125	Madigan AMC	Ft. Lewis	314.4	301.6	96
0089	Womack AMC	Ft. Bragg	199.4	148.2	74
0047	Eisenhower AMC	Ft. Gordon	165.8	134.4	81
0108	William Beaumont AMC	Ft. Bliss	181.5	128.0	71
0110	Darnall AMC	Ft. Hood	168.2	106.2	63
0032	Evans ACH	Ft. Carson	126.3	78.3	62
0048	Martin ACH	Ft. Benning	111.9	73.5	66
0060	Blanchfield ACH	Ft. Campbell	102.9	78.5	76
0123	Dewitt ACH	Ft. Belvoir	107.0	73.0	68
0061	Ireland ACH	Ft. Knox	68.3	39.2	57
0049	Winn ACH	Ft. Stewart	77.5	45.7	59
0075	L. Wood ACH	Ft. Leonard Wood	68.6	45.2	66
0098	Reynolds ACH	Ft. Sill	77.5	46.6	60
0105	Moncrief ACH	Ft. Jackson	48.5	33.0	68
0057	Irwin ACH	Ft. Riley	58.9	33.3	56
0005	Bassett ACH	Ft. Wainwright	47.4	26.5	56
0064	Bayne-Jones ACH	Ft. Polk	48.5	22.0	45
0086	Keller ACH	West Point	35.5	19.6	55
0131	Weed ACH	Ft. Irwin	24.9	11.7	47
Ambulatory					
0069	Kimbrough ACC	Ft. Meade	51.9	26.5	51
0121	McDonald AHC	Ft. Eustis	40.6	17.5	43
0330	Guthrie AHC	Ft. Drum	30.9	14.3	46
0008	R W Bliss AHC	Ft. Huachuca	23.9	8.3	35
0122	Kenner AHC	Ft. Lee	19.8	10.4	52
0058	Munson AHC	Ft. Leavenworth	21.0	9.3	44
0003	Lyster AHC	Ft. Rucker	13.8	8.3	60
0081	Occupational Health Clinic	Ft. Dix	8.8	5.3	60
0001	Fox AHC	Redstone Arsenal	7.4	6.3	85

[a] Excluding the costs of prescription ingredients.

Table A.4
Comparison of Navy FY 2007 MEPRS Stepped-Down A and B Expenses Against MERHCF and PPS Earnings

Parent DMIS ID	Facility	Stepped-Down MEPRS A & B Expenses ($M)[a]	PPS and MERHCF Earnings ($M)[a]	Earnings Share (%)
Inpatient				
0029	NMC San Diego	430.9	386.7	90
0124	NMC Portsmouth	401.2	290.2	72
0067	NNMC Bethesda	306.9	268.7	88
0024	NH Camp Pendleton	140.0	69.3	50
0039	NH Jacksonville	125.2	79.9	64
0038	NH Pensacola	96.6	69.7	72
0091	NH Camp Lejeune	120.5	73.3	61
0126	NH Bremerton	94.6	51.2	54
0104	NH Beaufort	43.8	23.4	54
0030	NH Twentynine Palms	43.3	16.4	38
0028	NH Lemoore	36.2	15.1	42
0127	NH Oak Harbor	33.4	17.1	51
0092	NH Cherry Point	27.2	13.8	51
Ambulatory				
0056	NHC Great Lakes	59.6	28.0	47
0100	NHC New England	54.2	18.6	34
0280	NHC Hawaii	29.9	15.3	51
0118	NH Corpus Christi	22.5	9.0	40
0103	NH Charleston	15.4	7.0	46
0385	NHC Quantico	19.9	9.2	46
0306	NHC Annapolis	9.6	6.2	65
0068	NHC Patuxent River	12.0	4.2	35

[a] Excluding the costs of prescription ingredients.

To construct these estimates, we assumed that MEPRS code DAA (prescription drug expenses) is stepped down to MEPRS codes A and B (inpatient and outpatient care expenses) only. However, some DAA costs could actually be stepped down to other MEPRS codes (for example, to dental care). For most MTFs, this assumption does not substantially affect the earnings-to-expenses ratio.

Table A.5 tallies the results of our revenue and expense calculations for CONUS AFMS MTFs.[1] For each type of MTF (inpatient or ambulatory), we list the DMIS identifier and facility name, ordered from highest to lowest total expenditures. The MILPERS column shows the total cost paid with DHP funds. These figures are estimates, based on the end strength of military personnel assigned (officer and enlisted) to each MTF, as listed in the 2007 President's Budget, multiplied by their average compensation, including regular pay, special pay, and bonuses.

The data in the Facility and Care columns under Expenses and in the Local column under Reimbursements were based on FY 2007 obligations data we received AFMOA.[2] Obligations are organized by program element codes (PECs), and then by Element of Expense Identification Codes. The facility costs are the sum of PECs 86276F, 86278F, 87779F, 87795F, and 87796F, which provide for facilities restoration, modernization, and sustainment, as well as base communications and operations. Care costs are the sum of PECs 87700F and 87701F, which fund defense medical centers, hospitals, and clinics,[3] as well as PEC 87715F, which funds dental care. From these sums, we subtract total expenditures on prescription drugs by MTF.

Local reimbursements are recorded as negative numbers in code 599 in the Air Force Surgeon General's budget database for PEC 87700F. The negative number indicates revenue—i.e., a negative expenditure. This means that funding is coming into the MTF from an external source, such as VHA, for care provided at the MTF. The MTF can spend this funding. Hence, local funding represents both expenditure on care and its reimbursement. We list this funding as a positive number.

The final column of the table shows the percentage of care-related expenses that is covered by revenues.

---

[1]   In this report, revenue and earnings are synonymous.

[2]   Obligations data are broken out by operating budget account number; some MTFs encompass more than one account number. We built a translation matrix to convert these into MTFs.

[3]   Although local reimbursements are for patient care, they are not included in the "care" column here.

Table A.5
Comparison of Air Force FY 2007 Estimated Obligations Against Local, PPS, and MERHCF Earnings

| DMIS ID | Unit | Installation | Expenses | | | | Local (expenses and revenue)[b] | Revenue | | | Total Revenue | Expenses Covered by Revenue (%) |
			MILPERS	Facility	Care[a,b]	Total Expenses		PPS	MERHCF[a]			
Inpatient												
0117	59th MDW	Lackland AFB	274.7	47.3	164.8	518.0	31.2	244.3	112.7	388.3	75.0
0095	60th MDG	Travis AFB	129.3	21.8	41.2	201.7	9.4	94.6	48.4	152.3	75.5
0014	88th MDG	Wright Patterson AFB	104.7	10.0	84.3	199.0	0.0	73.4	36.3	109.6	55.1
0042	81st MDG	Keesler AFB	121.4	8.7	47.5	180.1	2.6	24.5	13.9	41.0	22.8
0066	79th MDG	Andrews AFB	67.8	13.0	49.2	134.8	4.8	36.4	13.0	54.2	40.2
0079	96th MDG	Eglin AFB	73.1	7.0	47.5	127.6	0.0	45.9	12.1	58.0	45.5
0120	3rd MDG	Elmendorf AFB	65.9	13.0	17.5	106.0	9.7	42.0	5.9	57.5	54.2
0073	99th MDG Hospital	O'Callaghan AFB	63.1	1.6	28.8	105.3	11.9	37.4	9.5	58.9	55.9
0033	10th MDG	Air Force Academy	47.7	10.7	36.5	96.1	1.1	29.0	7.3	37.4	38.9
0006	1st MDG	Langley AFB	55.6	4.9	29.2	91.5	1.9	25.4	3.4	30.7	33.6
0053	366th MDG	Mountain Home AFB	20.4	0.6	9.4	31.2	0.8	8.2	1.1	10.2	32.7
Ambulatory												
0055	375th MDG	Scott AFB	42.9	4.6	33.1	84.3	3.8	11.5	3.5	18.8	22.3
0045	56th MDG	Luke AFB	26.4	27.4	13.5	69.0	1.6	9.7	3.3	14.5	21.1
0078	55th MDG	Offutt AFB	35.0	1.9	20.5	59.4	1.9	12.9	3.5	18.3	30.8
0009	6th MDG	Macdill AFB	38.3	3.6	12.7	58.5	3.8	11.3	5.4	20.5	35.1
0113	12th MDG	Randolph AFB	17.1	13.5	22.2	53.3	0.5	6.6	1.7	8.8	16.6
0043	82nd MDG	Sheppard AFB	28.0	6.2	13.7	49.2	1.2	9.1	2.8	13.1	26.7
0083	21st MDG	Peterson AFB	23.9	5.7	10.8	41.3	0.9	7.5	1.3	9.7	23.5
0252	72nd MDG	Tinker AFB	22.9	1.4	10.4	36.1	1.5	8.7	1.6	11.8	32.7
0096	305th MDG	Mcguire AFB	18.2	3.1	11.2	33.9	1.3	6.7	1.0	9.0	26.6
0010	355th MDG	Davis Monthan AFB	19.5	3.7	8.9	32.1	0.0	8.0	2.1	10.1	31.6
0051	314th MDG	Little Rock AFB	14.0	9.2	7.6	31.8	1.0	4.8	0.9	6.7	21.0

Table A.5—Continued

DMIS ID	Unit	Installation	Expenses MILPERS	Expenses Facility	Care[a,b]	Total Expenses	Local (expenses and revenue)[b]	Revenue PPS	Revenue MERHCF[a]	Total Revenue	Expenses Covered by Revenue (%)
0326	15th MDG	Hickam AFB	13.9	2.4	13.5	30.1	0.3	4.4	0.3	5.0	16.6
0119	78th MDG	Robins AFB	17.8	1.4	9.1	29.5	1.1	6.1	0.9	8.1	27.6
0366	2nd MDG	Barksdale AFB	18.8	0.6	8.4	29.2	1.4	5.1	1.0	7.6	25.9
0004	92nd MDG	Fairchild AFB	10.2	10.8	6.3	28.3	0.9	4.1	1.8	6.9	24.3
0112	42nd MDG	Maxwell AFB	13.4	2.3	10.8	28.2	1.6	7.5	1.7	10.8	38.4
0101	20th MDG	Shaw AFB	17.5	3.3	6.4	27.8	0.6	4.7	0.8	6.1	22.0
0062	325th MDG	Tyndall AFB	15.9	1.2	8.7	26.9	1.0	4.8	1.4	7.2	27.0
0128	75th MDG	Hill AFB	17.1	0.8	6.8	26.1	1.4	7.3	1.1	9.8	37.5
0046	45th MDG	Patrick AFB	13.8	1.5	7.3	25.9	3.3	5.0	3.3	11.6	44.9
7139	377th MDG	Kirtland AFB	18.8	3.0	3.1	25.0	0.2	5.3	3.0	8.5	33.8
0413	436th MDG	Dover AFB	16.0	2.7	4.9	24.9	1.3	5.2	1.4	7.9	31.8
0090	1st Special Ops MDG	Hurlburt AFB	16.7	0.9	6.3	24.1	0.2	5.7	0.6	6.6	27.3
0036	9th MDG	Beale AFB	18.9	0.8	3.8	23.6	0.1	3.0	0.8	4.0	16.9
0013	7th MDG	Dyess AFB	15.5	0.7	6.6	23.3	0.5	4.4	0.7	5.7	24.4
0084	49th MDG	Holloman AFB	15.3	1.3	5.5	22.5	0.3	4.0	1.2	5.4	24.2
0287	579th MDG	Bolling AFB	17.3	0.4	4.3	22.2	0.2	3.9	0.2	4.3	19.3
0015	437th MDG	Charleston AFB	13.7	1.9	5.6	21.9	0.7	3.8	0.5	5.1	23.2
0019	23rd MDG	Moody AFB	12.8	2.1	6.3	21.4	0.3	2.8	0.9	3.9	18.3
0395	95th MDG	Edwards AFB	14.5	1.3	5.3	21.2	0.2	2.9	0.4	3.6	16.8
0094	4th MDG	Seymour Johnson AFB	15.3	0.8	4.3	20.9	0.5	4.2	1.2	5.9	28.2
0076	5th MDG	Minot AFB	12.8	1.7	5.1	19.9	0.3	3.6	0.3	4.3	21.4
0050	43rd MDG	Pope AFB	14.5	0.8	4.4	19.8	0.1	3.6	0.2	3.8	19.2
0335	90th MDG	F.E. Warren AFB	14.2	0.6	4.5	19.8	0.5	2.7	0.6	3.7	18.9
7200	22nd MDG	McConnell AFB	12.3	1.3	5.1	19.3	0.5	3.8	1.1	5.4	28.0
0106	62nd MDG	McChord AFB	14.1	1.4	3.2	19.2	0.5	3.7	0.9	5.1	26.6

Table A.5—Continued

DMIS ID	Unit	Installation	Expenses					Revenue			Expenses Covered by Revenue (%)
			MILPERS	Facility	Care[a,b]	Total Expenses	Local (expenses and revenue)[b]	PPS	MERHCF[a]	Total Revenue	
0077	28th MDG	Ellsworth AFB	12.0	0.6	6.1	19.1	0.4	3.6	0.4	4.3	22.8
0018	341st MDG	Malmstrom AFB	10.2	3.8	4.5	19.0	0.4	3.6	0.6	4.6	24.0
0338	509th MDG	Whiteman AFB	12.4	0.8	5.2	18.7	0.3	3.6	0.6	4.5	24.2
0059	30th MDG	Vandenberg AFB	11.2	0.9	5.7	17.9	0.1	2.8	0.9	3.8	21.3
0129	17th MDG	Goodfellow AFB	8.9	4.8	3.7	17.5	0.2	2.7	0.6	3.5	19.7
0085	27th MDG	Cannon AFB	11.4	0.3	4.8	16.6	0.1	2.6	0.4	3.1	18.6
0310	354th MDG	Eielson AFB	10.7	1.0	3.5	15.4	0.1	2.3	0.0	2.5	16.0
0356	319th MDG	Grand Forks AFB	9.8	1.1	3.7	15.0	0.3	2.2	0.3	2.7	18.3
0203	460th MDG	Buckley AFB	6.6	1.6	5.0	14.3	1.1	1.9	2.3	5.3	37.0
0093	66th MDG	Hanscom AFB	9.4	1.4	2.9	13.7	0.0	1.9	1.2	3.0	22.2
0364	14th MDG	Columbus AFB	8.7	1.2	3.1	13.3	0.3	2.0	1.0	3.3	25.0
0074	97th MDG	Altus AFB	7.6	2.0	3.3	13.0	0.2	1.8	0.3	2.4	18.2
0248	61st MDS	Los Angeles AFB	8.0	1.5	3.4	12.8	0.0	2.4	1.2	3.7	28.6
0097	47th MDG	Laughlin AFB	8.2	0.3	1.9	10.6	0.2	1.5	0.6	2.3	21.6
0114	71st MDG	Vance AFB	7.4	0.9	1.8	10.2	0.2	1.5	0.4	2.1	20.6

[a] Data based on FY 2007 obligations data from AFMOA.
[b] Excludes prescription ingredient costs.

Readiness Full-Time Equivalents by Service

Tables B.1 through B.3 show the number of clinician and nurse FTEs spent on readiness activities in each service. They also show the percentage of FTEs recorded as deployments versus all other readiness activities.

Table B.1
AFMS Clinician and Nurse Annual Readiness FTEs, by Year

	FY 2001	FY 2002	FY 2003	FY 2004	FY 2005	FY 2006	FY 2007
Clinicians							
Total readiness FTEs	126	196	235	260	324	324	346
Deployment FTEs	32	112	139	100	135	135	153
Percentage recorded as deployment	25	57	59	38	42	42	44
Nurses							
Total readiness FTEs	77	140	175	185	250	226	250
Deployment FTEs	11	73	101	77	124	109	132
Percentage	14	52	58	42	50	48	53

Table B.2
Army Clinician and Nurse Annual Readiness FTEs, by Year

	FY 2001	FY 2002	FY 2003	FY 2004	FY 2005	FY 2006	FY 2007
Clinicians							
Total readiness FTEs	245	266	448	423	440	465	389
Deployment FTEs	44	73	273	260	288	342	284
Percentage recorded as deployment	18	28	61	62	65	74	73
Nurses							
Total readiness FTEs	85	110	309	256	273	344	237
Deployment FTEs	11	23	231	158	205	284	173
Percentage	13	21	75	62	75	83	73

Table B.3
Navy Clinician and Nurse Annual Readiness FTEs, by Year

	FY 2001	FY 2002	FY 2003	FY 2004	FY 2005	FY 2006	FY 2007
Clinicians							
Total readiness FTEs	137	134	210	162	168	217	215
Deployment FTE	1	12	91	55	72	130	136
Percentage recorded as deployment	1	9	43	34	43	60	63
Nurses							
Total readiness FTEs	101	101	198	123	131	161	157
Deployment FTEs	0.4	13	114	57	75	109	105
Percentage	0	13	58	47	57	67	67

Prospective Payment System

Because of increases in purchased care expenditures and decreased workloads at the services' MTFs, OASD(HA) initiated PPS in FY 2003, applying the first adjustments to the services' budgets in FY 2005. The PPS methodology established a baseline for U.S. MTFs for both inpatient and ambulatory workloads using FY 2003 workload data. This baseline was compared to forecast workloads beginning in FY 2005, and the differences between the two data sets were calculated each year for each type of procedure. Funding adjustments based on these calculations were phased in over four years, with incremental adjustments of 25 percent of the calculated amount in FY 2004, 50 percent in FY 2005, 75 percent in FY 2006, and 100 percent in FY 2007. The baseline year was changed to FY 2007 for the FY 2008 calculation.

PPS addresses only direct care delivered at MTFs within the 50 states; Alaska and Hawaii are reimbursed at higher rates, because their costs are higher than those of other CONUS MTFs. The ambulatory workload is defined as procedures recorded in SADRs (measured by RVUs). The inpatient workload is defined as procedures recorded in SIDRs (measured as RWPs). Prescriptions, pathology, radiology, and other ancillary services are not funded through PPS, but through traditional budgeting.

Prices for RWPs and RVUs are based on national CMAC rates, which are then tailored to the location of each MTF. RWPs are priced using CMAC rates tailored to local wage indices and Indirect Medical Adjustment factors, which range from about 4 percent to more than 56 percent of costs. Costs are divided into professional and institutional components of 20 percent and 80 percent, respectively. In comparison, a civilian institution would bill each of these costs separately. At MHS teaching hospitals, an indirect medical care cost is added. MHS-wide earnings in FY 2008 averaged about $11,100 per RWP, with some variation among the services. For example, the AFMS average was $11,825.

RVUs are based on CMAC rates, segmented by specialty and adjusted for a local wage index. For example, the value for an emergency room procedure would be different from that for a primary care visit. Except for emergency room visits, institutional costs are not included in RVU earnings. In contrast, a civilian institution would bill for both the professional component (an RVU), and the institutional component (called an Ambulatory Procedures Classification). FY 2008 earnings under PPS averaged just over $70 per RVU, with little variation among services.[1]

---

[1] OASD(HA) PPS spreadsheet data.

Unlike the MERHCF earnings calculation,[2] PPS does not use MEPRS cost data (actual costs) from the MTFs to establish earnings.[3] The use of CMAC rates has been a point of contention between the services and TMA because PPS rates are generally lower than what it actually costs the MTF to provide care. PPS also calculates earnings for the mental health workload using bed days in much the same manner as it calculates inpatient RWPs.

After the workload forecasts are made, the services' budgets are adjusted upward or downward, depending on whether the workload is expected to be higher or lower than the base year. An adjustment is also made in May of each year that is based on the workload during the previous 12 months (a rolling 12-month average). If workload is lower than forecast, the funding to that service is reduced. Reductions are made to the O&M and MILPERS budgets based on workload forecasts, but the services can apply the reductions to either appropriation during the POM process. For midyear adjustments, the calculated increase or decrease is applied only to the O&M budget because MILPERS cannot be adjusted during the budget execution year.[4]

The Centers for Medicare and Medicaid Services, along with the American Medical Association, periodically update the RVUs. For example, in FY 2007, they reviewed five years' worth of RVUs, which resulted in significant changes in the work content and rates for some RVUs. Most evaluation and management codes were given higher RVU credits that reflected the skills medical professionals used (rather than the procedure codes, which relate to the equipment used and what they did to the patient).[5] These rate increases ranged from 0.6 percent for ophthalmology to more than 22 percent for emergency room visits; primary care was more than 17.6 percent higher. However, to achieve a balanced budget, OASD(HA) applied a budget neutrality factor of 0.8994 to the new RVU values; this resulted in a net increase of 10 percent for emergency room visits; a reduction of 9.5 percent for ophthalmology; and a 5.8 percent increase for primary care.[6]

The overall effects of PPS adjustments in FY 2007 were as follows:

- The value of the Army's workload increased by $100 million, but because about 60 percent of its funding is O&M, the service received an additional $60 million.
- The Navy's budget was reduced by about $20 million.
- The value of AFMS's workload fell by about $80 million, but because only about 28 percent of its workload is O&M funded, its budget was reduced by $21 million.

---

[2] See Appendix D for more information on MERHCF.

[3] See Chapter Four for more information on MEPRS.

[4] See Chapter Three for details on MHS appropriations.

[5] Evaluation and management services refer to visits and consultations provided by physicians or residents under their supervision. Each of these services is assigned a current procedure terminology code for billing purposes. These codes were developed by the American Medical Association and implemented by the Health Care Financing Administration (now called the Centers for Medicare and Medicaid Services) in 1992, as part of the sweeping changes required by the resource-based Medicare fee schedule payment system. Like all current procedure terminology codes, evaluation and management codes are "universal" and used by Medicare, Medicaid, and most other payers to process claims for the professional services of physicians. Because visit and consultation services are high-volume physician activities, the codes for evaluation and management are the ones physicians use most frequently in daily practice. See the American Association of Medical Colleges' web page.

[6] A budget neutrality factor was established to reduce total costs to the amount available in the budget.

These changes were based on a 75-percent adjustment factor relative to the baseline year of FY 2003. In FY 2008, the PPS adjustment will be 100 percent of the difference between the new baseline (FY 2007) and the rolling 12-month average for the mid–FY 2008 adjustment.

Keesler AFB hospital was not included in these calculations because of the effects of Hurricane Katrina, which essentially shut down the hospital's inpatient capabilities and severely reduced its ambulatory capabilities in FY 2006.

As a future initiative, OASD(HA) is investigating whether to incorporate Ambulatory Procedures Classifications into the PPS methodology (possibly in FY 2010), thereby possibly raising the value of an outpatient RVU. However, the professional component will be reduced because its value is based partly on the assumption that the visit is to a physician's office. (These costs would not exist in an institutional setting.) This change would capture the cost of ASCs, which are becoming more numerous as MHS hospitals are converting to ASCs.

Also, after the NPI system is fully implemented, OASD(HA) may use this information in its PPS calculations to further refine the identification of workload credit.[7] NPI will identify who performs work, in addition to where the work is performed. Thus, a provider assigned to another service's facility could at least receive credit for the professional portion of the work performed elsewhere, thereby capturing earnings that would either be lost to the parent service or be attributed to another service under the current system. Thus, each service would get credit for the workload of its surgeons on loan to other services or to civilian hospitals. In addition, NPI will allow more accurate tracking of workload within an MTF.

---

[7]   NPI assigns each provider a unique identification number that can be used to identify all workload he or she performs. Nurses and support staff will not have NPIs, so their external workload will not be captured for their parent service.

Medicare-Eligible Retiree Health Care Fund

The FY 2001 National Defense Authorization Act directed the establishment of the Medicare-Eligible Retiree Health Care Fund to reimburse MTFs for this care beginning on October 1, 2002. Prior to that date, care for Medicare-eligible beneficiaries was financed through annual congressional appropriations for space available care in MTFs (DoD, 2005). Although called "Medicare eligible," the population covered includes military retirees, their family members, and survivors of military personnel, not just retirees aged 65 and over. Altogether, nearly 2 million people are eligible under MERHCF.

MERHCF receives funds from three sources: the U.S. Treasury, via an actuarial liability of $13 billion annually for 50 years; DoD, via an annual contribution of about $11 billion; and investment earnings from the U.S. Treasury on funds in excess of annual expenditures. In FY 2008, it was estimated that the fund would pay out a total of $8.3 billion; $6.6 billion for purchased health care and $1.7 billion as reimbursements to the services for care provided at MTFs.

Much like PPS, annual MERHCF earnings are based on forecasts of MTF workloads. These forecasts are based on actual workloads in prior years. MERHCF reimburses the services for inpatient procedures, ambulatory procedures, and prescriptions filled.

Unlike PPS, MERHCF reimburses all MTFs, whether in the 50 states or overseas. MERHCF payments are based on the actual costs MTFs report in MEPRS, not derived from other sources, such as CMAC rates used in PPS.

In addition to the dollar-for-dollar reimbursement of all costs MTFs incur for each procedure, the MERHCF population provides a better workload mix for training and retaining the currency of critical-care specialists (surgeons, operating room and intensive care nurses, and technicians). The MERHCF population is older than the active-duty population and its dependents and tends to have more-complicated health-care needs. In fact, 28 percent of all inpatient AFMS performed in FY 2007 was for the MERHCF population. In FY 2007, AFMS received $577 million in total earnings from the fund, of which $249 million was for prescription ingredients. The Army earned $614 million (including $168 million for prescription ingredients), while the Navy earned $404 million (including $133 million for prescription ingredients) in FY 2007.

Consolidation of Wilford Hall Medical Center and Brooke Army Medical Center

Background

In its final report to the President, the 2005 Defense Base Realignment and Closure Commission recommended

> realign[ing] Lackland Air Force Base, TX, by relocating the inpatient medical function of the 59th Medical Wing (Wilford Hall Medical Center) to the Brooke Army Medical Center, Fort Sam Houston, TX, establishing it as the San Antonio Regional Military Medical Center [SAMMC], and converting Wilford Hall Medical Center into an ambulatory care center. (BRAC, 2005)

The commission's rationale for this included the desirability of

- transforming legacy medical infrastructure into a modernized joint operational medical facility
- reducing excess capacity in the San Antonio market
- maintaining the level of care for beneficiaries
- enhancing opportunities for provider currency
- maintaining surge capacity.

The BRAC Commission envisioned one unified medical center, SAMMC, with two campuses, north and south, delivering high-quality, cost-effective health care in world-class facilities while providing wartime readiness support and training. All BRAC actions must be completed by the end of FY 2011 (September 30, 2011). While the staffs at both WHMC and BAMC are working in earnest to complete all actions required for a smooth transition, examining the creation of SAMMC and understanding its implications for AFMS provide insights into the challenges that AFMS is likely to face in the future.

Facilities

WHMC (59th Medical Wing) is the flagship of AFMS. It has more than 200 beds, performs nearly one-half of all AFMS inpatient procedures and about 10 percent of ambulatory procedures, and earns more than one-quarter of the total AFMS funding from PPS and MERHCF. The next largest AFMS hospital is at Travis AFB, California, which conducted less than one-third of the number of inpatient procedures that WHMC did in FY 2007. WHMC supplied about one-third of the AFMS surgeons and nurses who deployed in FY 2007 and is the only Level I trauma center AFMS operates. WHMC clearly plays a critical role in AFMS inpatient capabilities.

BAMC performs more inpatient procedures than any other Army MTF (about 16 percent of the total), performs about 7 percent of the ambulatory procedures, and earns about 13 percent of total Army funding from PPS and MERHCF. However, three other major Army hospitals conduct a significant amount of inpatient work: Walter Reed Army Medical Center in Washington, D.C. (13 percent of the total inpatient workload), which will be merging with Bethesda National Naval Medical Center in Maryland; Tripler Army Medical Center in Hawaii (12 percent); and Madigan Army Medical Center in Washington (also 12 percent). Overall, the Army performs almost three times the number of inpatient procedures as the Air Force.

In FY 2006 the DoD beneficiary population in San Antonio was 213,168. A total of 144,056 were enrolled in TRICARE, including 60,876 at WHMC; 23,289 at the clinic at Randolph AFB; 50,672 at BAMC; and 9,212 at TRICARE network providers. There were also approximately 9,000 transient students at Lackland AFB and 4,500 at Ft. Sam Houston. The decision to make the north campus the inpatient facility was based on the fact that BAMC was newer, capable of supporting more than 400 beds, while WHMC was aging and would have required replacement to continue as a tertiary-care medical facility.

The vision for SAMMC's end state is the largest inpatient facility in DoD and one of the largest outpatient facilities. SAMMC North will have 425 inpatient beds, including 116 intensive-care unit beds; a Level 1 trauma center and emergency room; pediatric and surgical subspecialty clinics; facilities for labor, delivery, and recovery, as well as neonatal and pediatric intensive care; facilities for bone marrow transplants; new centers of excellence in cardiovascular services, maternal-child health, and battlefield health and trauma; and an expanded burn unit (the Institute of Surgical Research). SAMMC South will provide primary care, 24/7 urgent care for trainees, pediatric and surgical subspecialty clinics, and a new center of excellence for eye care. There is an initiative to fund the construction of an ASC, which will expand the initial scope of services intended for SAMMC South.

Consolidation Issues

The major issues associated with consolidation of the two facilities can be grouped into five general areas: training, governance, human resources, resourcing, and workload attribution.

Prior to the BRAC decision, the Army and Air Force had been combining their GME programs in San Antonio. During the 2010–2011 academic year, all SAMMC GME programs will fall under the SAMMC Health Education Committee. The final two GME programs, orthopedic surgery and general surgery, will be combined in 2011. The GME program will support 343 Air Force, 264 Army, and one Navy resident, as well as the Health Professionals Scholarship Program and Uniformed Services University of the Health Sciences students. The training of enlisted medical specialties will also be combined, but this change will require greater coordination among the services. Unlike physician and nurse medical specialties, for which there are national training, examination, and licensure requirements (such as those prescribed by the American College of Graduate Medical Education and by such professional specialty associations as the American Board of Internal Medicine), enlisted medical training is more specific to each service's unique approach to requirements, training, utilization, and career paths. Consequently, SAMMC has established an Enlisted Training Council to cross-train all Army medical Military Operational Specialties and AFSCs. The first group of enlisted specialties combined during FY 2008 included respiratory therapists, radiology technicians, laboratory technicians, pharmacy technicians, and patient administrators. Greater challenges in cross-training may emerge as enlisted personnel who work on inpatient wards and in outpatient clinics are identified for cross-training. The Army and Air Force have different approaches to the training and utilization of enlisted medics, corpsmen, licensed practical nurses, and ward staff support nurses. Standardized training of enlisted medical personnel, centralized at Ft. Sam Houston, is intended to simplify triservice enlisted training. However, as of the end of FY 2008, the individual services had yet to agree on training requirements and the minimum standard for skill qualification.

Another concern AFMS personnel expressed is ensuring that SAMMC has sufficient billets to train enough critical surgical, trauma, and emergency services specialists and corpsmen to support the rotation base and to provide real-world trauma experience similar to that available at WHMC. The WHMC critical-care workload provided training opportunities that allowed the Air Force to assume expanded roles, including operating critical-care in-theater hospitals in Bagram and Balad, which were not part of its typical responsibilities. With the loss of WHMC as a regional Level 1 trauma and emergency room referral center, it will be critical to share the workload at SAMMC North in a manner that allows Air Force medical personnel to acquire and maintain required skills.

The final governance structure of SAMMC has not yet been determined. As of the end of FY 2008, there was an interim governance structure, headed by a general officer council comprising the WHMC and BAMC commanders and a senior executive steering committee with five executive staff members from each of the two facilities. The department chairs and multiple functional working groups report to the steering committee. The San Antonio Medical BRAC Integration Office includes a BRAC codirector from each of the facilities and is responsible for a cross-functional team of experts dedicated to helping the medical treatment facilities in the San Antonio Multi-Service Market integrate in accordance with BRAC law. Management is focused on the areas of logistics, resource management, manpower, and information management. Other functions include the typical administrative areas, as well as facility and equipment planners, clinical mission planners, and movement coordinators. AFMS personnel expressed concern that the unified governance structure would provide insufficient leader-development opportunities. While the south campus will house an ASC, as well as primary care and specialty care clinics, the vast majority of training, teaching, and GME program management will be located on the north campus. Ensuring that AFMS has an appropriate say, has necessary representation, and is provided sufficient leadership opportunities to identify and develop future clinical and administrative leaders will be critical to the ongoing success of Air Force medicine.

Human resources will also be challenging as the management of military and civilian personnel combine across services, not only at SAMMC but also at other MTFs being merged in response to the BRAC. For military personnel, the considerations include differences in the services' training standards, the lack of a direct match between Military Operational Specialties and AFSCs, service-specific expectations for job performance and competency, specific staffing models, supervision, predeployment training requirements, and deployment lengths. Issues for civilian personnel include perceived discrepancies between equivalent job series, two civilian service-affiliated workforces instead of one, and differences in the use of civilians. The current plan is not to use a single service's civilian personnel system but to allow the civilian workforce to retain its current status and modify job descriptions to standardize them so that duties are not location specific. Thus, Air Force civilians will retain their Air Force civilian career status when their clinical duties are relocated to SAMMC North. This approach could cause administrative and recruiting challenges. Additionally, because the Army generally uses more civilians at MTFs than either the Air Force or the Navy, there will have to be some military-cultural accommodation, for example, when young military nurses work on wards where senior Army civilian nurses are in charge. Furthermore, AFMS may be required to support its share of staffing commitments and, when unforeseen deployments occur, may have to become more flexible about hiring civilians.

Equitable resourcing of the two facilities and their staffs and workload attribution issues are interwoven. Workload funding is based on RVUs and RWPs. However, in San Antonio, AFMS supported many other missions directly and indirectly using resources earned through PPS and MERHCF at WHMC. It is not clear how funding will flow from the DHP to and between the two services to fund the necessary infrastructure that extends beyond direct patient care. All the high-value workload, RWPs, will be earned and reported at SAMMC North, and AFMS military and civilian personnel will perform a significant share of that work. Adjustments may be needed to ensure that sufficient resources are provided to maintain and sustain both the north and south campuses. Resourcing AFMS in San Antonio is of course a bigger issue than simply providing for adequate funding of SAMMC South. Until SAMMC is fully implemented and until integration is complete, including MILCON at both the north and south campuses, the true funding requirements will not be known. Not only will there be direct costs to support AFMS missions in San Antonio, but there may also be second-order consequences that directly affect AFMS and may require additional resources not related to the workload. For instance, when AFMS loses direct control of the inpatient workload and the Level 1 trauma center that had been at WHMC, providers assigned to other MTFs that had rotated through WHMC to maintain currency and produce workload may have to be sent to the Center for the Sustainment of Trauma and Readiness Skills to get enough experience to ensure currency. The opportunity costs of reducing direct care and incurring temporary-duty travel will likely increase the cost of readiness and health-care delivery. AFMS personnel expressed concern that the loss of the Air Force's largest medical facility would reduce the Air Force's flexibility, autonomy, and direct authority to accomplish traditional Title 10 missions.

Understanding the direct funding resource implications for AFMS of the creation of SAMMC is of critical importance to AFMS. Historically, WHMC has achieved a relatively high level of PPS and MERHCF earnings, covering approximately 72 percent of its overall operating costs, compared to an average of 57 percent for all Air Force hospitals. PPS and MERHCF cover an average of only about 30 percent of the operating costs of AFMS outpatient clinics and ASCs. To estimate the effects on AFMS earnings of the consolidation of WHMC and BAMC, we obtained data on the current costs and earnings for both locations for FY 2007 (see Table E.1).

Next, we realigned the same earnings and expenses according to the general guidelines briefed to us during our visits to both locations. Some ambulatory workload migrates between

Table E.1
Wilford Hall Medical Center and Brooke Army Medical Center
Earnings and Expenses

	WHMC	BAMC
Expenses		
MILPERS	274,691	126,110
O&M		
Civilian pay and benefits	52,983	100,051
Other O&M	255,406	278,242
Total O&M	308,389	378,293
Total expenses	583,080	504,403
Earnings		
PPS/MERHCF	366,714	336,925
MERHCF prescriptions (MILPERS)	1,657	331
MERHCF prescriptions (O&M)	19,719	14,511
Total earnings	388,091	351,768
Earnings less expenses	(194,989)	(152,635)
GWOT expenses[a]	22,217	65,170

NOTES: Because of rounding, totals may not sum precisely.
Amounts in FY 2007 $000s.

[a] Not included above.

campuses, but the major change is the shift of all inpatient workload to SAMMC North. Table E.2 shows the effect on earnings and costs for each service after the merger, including the forecast BRAC savings in manpower for the Air Force at SAMMC South. We assumed that all workload (and therefore, earnings) performed at SAMMC North would be credited to the Army, while the workload and earnings at SAMMC South would be attributed to the Air Force. The net estimated effect of the merger is a reduction to AFMS of almost $250 million, even with the postulated manpower savings.

Alternative approaches could be used to attribute earnings and costs to each facility. For cost accumulation under MEPRS, unique codes have been established to allow personnel to allocate their time to either campus. The implementation of NPI in the future would allow the providers to associate their efforts with their parent service; however, NPI implementation would not account for nonprovider contributions to the workload.

Without changes in resource allocation methodologies that are primarily based on workload, AFMS could lose a disproportionate share of resources. The consolidation could have a significant effect on AFMS funding in the POM because PPS and MERHCF funding is based on projections of the workloads of each service. In developing funding guidance for each service, projected workload earnings would be inaccurate, since the Air Force would not get full credit for the projected workload at SAMMC North, while the Army would not get credit for the work of its personnel at SAMMC South, but would be funded for the work of AFMS providers at SAMMC North. Although the O&M funds could be realigned during the FY 2012 and later execution years, the MILPERS accounts must be accurately forecast in the President's Budget, because MILPERS funding cannot be realigned among services during budget execution. In addition, accurate workload forecasts are needed to permit necessary personnel

Table E.2
Estimated SAMMC Postintegration
Earnings and Expenses

	SAMMC	
	South	North
Expenses		
MILPERS	274,691	126,110
136 MILPERS reduction	(13,457)	N/A
O&M		
Civilian pay and benefits	52,983	100,051
104 civilian personnel reduction	(7,080)	N/A
Other O&M[a]	255,406	278,242
Total O&M	301,309	378,293
Total expenses	562,543	504,403
Earnings		
PPS/MERHCF	100,616	603,024
MERHCF prescriptions (MILPERS)	1,657	331
MERHCF prescriptions (O&M)	19,719	14,511
Total earnings	121,993	617,866
Revenue minus expenses	(440,551)	113,463
Preintegration earnings minus expenses	(194,989)	(152,635)

NOTES: Because of rounding, totals may not sum precisely.
Amounts in FY 2007 $000s.

[a] We assume patient care O&M remains with the current
location; in effect, migration of both inpatient and ambulatory
workload between locations would require a reevaluation of
O&M care costs, such as surgical supplies. Estimating these cost
migrations is beyond the scope of this study.

reassignments throughout AFMS and the Army. A solution must be found for the FY 2012
POM preparation exercise (beginning in 2010). One option that should be considered is to
suspend normal PPS and MERHCF calculations and maintain "shadow" workload forecasts
for the first year or two until the allocation of workloads between the two campuses stabilizes,
allowing better calculations of MILPERS costs. Under this option, baseline funding could
be provided (both O&M and MILPERS) at both locations as an interim measure. A similar
action to suspend normal PPS and MERHCF was taken to adjust funding for Keesler after
Hurricane Katrina.

Tied closely with resourcing is proper workload attribution. As discussed in Chapter
Four, AFMS is continuing to implement DMHRSi. It is important to implement this system
at SAMMC as soon as possible.[1] While MEPRS is currently reporting workload and labor at
SAMMC with special codes established for each location, MEPRS does not provide sufficient
detail to document the workload of AFMS providers and staff assigned to Lackland but doing

---

[1]   DMHRSi implementation was completed AFMS-wide as of September 30, 2009; the Army and Navy had previously
implemented the system.

most of their work at the north campus. MEPRS is designed to document loaned and borrowed military labor and civilian labor, but it does not differentiate the source (service) of the borrowed or loaned labor. Without documentation of the work AFMS personnel perform at SAMMC North, it could become increasingly difficult for AFMS to justify and defend Air Force medical missions and budgets. Fortunately, DMHRSi is able to track personnel working at any workstation in any facility, including service affiliations. Consequently, with more accurate data, AFMS leadership will be able to document the workloads of its medical personnel. DMHRSi is a significant improvement over MEPRS (if data are entered correctly) because it provides specific names, hours, and locations where work was performed. DMHRSi will permit tracking of ward staffing AFMS contributes to the north campus and, coupled with the Armed Forces Health Longitudinal Technology Application, will allow identification of provider visits and time spent in clinics, thereby documenting workload, efficiency, and the PPS value of work performed.

The challenges AFMS faces also include planning for the eventual realignment of inpatient services from SAMMC South to SAMMC North and the second-order implications. Although AFMS will still have the majority presence at SAMMC South, including some specialties offered only on the south campus and a robust ASC, inpatient care and associated training programs will be located on the north campus. Ensuring that AFMS remains an equal player or partner, with the opportunity to share the most senior leadership positions, is crucial to maintaining the visibility and status of AFMS.

Unless current workload-based resource allocations are modified, AFMS could find itself resource constrained after inpatient care is moved to the north campus and the Army receives the resources and PPS and MERHCF earnings for care delivered there. Given the extraordinary change that will occur, AFMS should work with OASD(HA) and TMA to suspend current workload-based resourcing processes until a mature steady-state operation is in place. Similar resource allocation challenges must be addressed at facilities that are being combined in the National Capital Region.

Efficiency-Wedge Reductions

In the FY 2005–2009 POM Update cycle, the Under Secretary of Defense (Comptroller) and the Director, Program Analysis and Evaluation, required the use of change proposals for moving funds within and between programs and submitting unfinanced requirements.[1] A key feature of the change proposal process was that no unfinanced requirements could be submitted without identifying equivalent proposed offsets within the fiscal guidance issued for the program.[2]

The DHP identified a large, unfinanced requirement across the FY 2005–2009 POM ($1.7 billion in FY 2005, and a total of $12.8 billion over FYs 2005–2009). Because it could identify only $1.2 billion of offsets within its fiscal guidance, several creative offsets were developed, including elimination of 5,000 unfilled DHP-funded MILPERS billets, the application of federal pricing to TRICARE retail pharmacies, and TRICARE benefit reform (increased enrollment fees, user fees, and copays for retirees and dependents). Even with these offsets, there was still a shortfall of $1.67 billion across the FY 2005–2009 POM.

TMA conducted a "valuation study" comparing the cost of producing health care in MTFs to the cost of equivalent private-sector care. Based on FY 2003 data, this study found that the cost of the care MTFs provided exceeded the cost to purchase equivalent care from the private sector by $3.7 billion, or 56 percent. This comparison excluded outpatient pharmacy costs, where the federal pricing structure gives MTFs a significant advantage over retail pharmacies. This study also found wide variations in the cost of care at individual MTFs. It estimated that, if underperforming MTFs could improve to within 25 percent of the mean cost per workload unit for other MTFs of similar size, efficiencies of $3.7 billion could be achieved, assuming stable workload.

These "MTF efficiencies" were included in the program change proposal to cover the remaining unfinanced requirement. The amounts for each FY were allocated to the Army, Navy, and Air Force based on their share of the $3.7 billion identified in the valuation study (see Table F.1).

Other proposed internal DHP offsets, federal pricing in TRICARE retail pharmacies, and the MTF efficiencies were subsequently accepted as offsets during the program and budget review and were implemented in Program Budget Decision 041R in the FY 2005 President's Budget cycle. For years beyond FY 2009, the FY 2009 adjustments were increased at the pro-

---

[1] Such change requests were called *program change proposals* for POM issues and *budget change proposals* for budget estimate submission issues.

[2] Most of the material in this appendix is based on Yow, undated.

jected rate of inflation. Adjusting for inflation, the MTF efficiencies required in FY 2009 represented 17.8 percent of the original $3.7 billion identified by the valuation study.

To account for these efficiencies, the military medical services elected to reduce their DHP O&M appropriations by the full amount rather than spread them over other appropriations. Because much of the cost of health care in MTFs is military labor, this decision resulted in large reductions to DHP O&M appropriations. The Army's MTF personnel are approximately 50 percent military, but those of the Air Force and Navy are approximately 80 percent military, so the effects on DHP O&M were particularly pronounced for these two services.

In the FY 2008–2013 POM cycle, several adjustments were made to the allocation of MTF efficiencies. First, the efficiencies were adjusted to account for savings already included in BRAC assumptions. For example, one location highlighted for potential efficiencies was the clinic at Pope Air Force Base, which was subsequently targeted for closure under BRAC. In addition, TMA completed a joint update of the valuation study with the military medical services that changed the proportionate shares of the assumed efficiencies. The results were incorporated into the FY 2008–2013 DHP POM and the FY 2008 President's Budget (see Table F.2).

However, the effects of the efficiency-wedge reductions were later offset by funding increases during the year of execution, so budgets actually increased in FYs 2006–2008. In FY 2009, the O&M budget was reduced by $323.8 million. Congress prohibited any further efficiency-wedge reductions in FY 2010 and later years. Chapter Three provides the congressional language on the efficiency wedge.

Table F.1
MTF Efficiencies Allocated to Each Service, FYs 2006–2009

Service	FY 2006	FY 2007	FY 2008	FY 2009
Army	29.8	82.1	142.5	227.6
Navy	30.6	84.4	149.5	239.0
Air Force	33.6	92.5	215.0	343.4
Total	94.0	259.0	507.0	810.0

Table F.2
MTF Efficiencies Allocated to Each Service, FYs 2008–2013 ($M)

Service	FY 2008	FY 2009	FY 2010	FY 2011	FY 2012	FY 2013
Army	142.3	227.3	164.1	155.1	158.3	161.5
Navy	146.5	234.2	219.5	226.1	232.9	240.0
Air Force	197.5	323.7	316.5	326.3	336.2	346.3
BRAC overlap	20.7	24.8	136.5	156.7	165.2	174.2
Total	507.0	810.0	836.6	864.2	892.6	922.0

Support to Landstuhl Regional Medical Center

AFMS has played an important and generally unrecognized role in the European Theater of Operations, providing approximately 300 military personnel to support health-care delivery at LRMC.[1]

The 435th Medical Group (MDG), headquartered at Ramstein AB, Germany, comprises five squadrons with approximately 800 assigned personnel. Four of the squadrons (435th Medical Support Squadron, 435th Dental Squadron, 435th Aerospace Medicine Squadron, and 435th Medical Operations Squadron), with 500 assigned personnel, are located at Ramstein AB. The other 300 personnel are assigned to 435th Medical Squadron (MDS), with duty at LRMC. LRMC accounts for AFMS personnel assigned to it as borrowed military manpower, but none of the workload they perform there is reported or credited to the 435th MDG activities at Ramstein. This occurs because MEPRS collects and reports workload where it is produced. The workload attributable to borrowed military manpower is not specifically identifiable because all sources of borrowed military manpower, including other unassigned Army Medical Department staff and volunteers, are reported together. In some cases, AFMS staff not specifically assigned to 435 MDS also work at LRMC, particularly to maintain currency.

The 435th MDS produces a significant amount of the total workload at LRMC. The staff of the 435 MDS at LRMC provided us data they extracted from the MHS Management Analysis and Reporting Tool database that describe workload LRMC reported in MEPRS for FY 2007. Table G.1 shows the total workload at LRMC and the estimated AFMS personnel share. The workload allocation was based on NPIs, where known. However, we excluded 36 inpatient and 103 outpatient NPIs that could not be identified as either Army or Air Force,

Table G.1
LRMC Total Workload and AFMS Portion

	Total LRMC	AFMS	Percentage AFMS
Inpatient providers	206	35	17
Outpatient providers	641	92	14
RWPs	9,977	2,229	22
Bed days	31,359	7,074	23
RVUs	351,993	66,753	19

---

[1] There is a memorandum of agreement between the 435th MDG and LRMC, but we were not able to obtain a copy because it was being revised.

so the AFMS share is probably understated. As Table G.1 shows, AFMS produced at least 22 percent of the RWPs (inpatient workload), 23 percent of the bed days, and 19 percent of the RVUs (outpatient workload).

The equivalent earnings for AFMS under PPS and MERHCF would have been at least $26 million (since we could not identify all NPIs). However, since PPS is not applied to MTFs outside the United States, most of these earnings are hypothetical. For FY 2007, the entire MERHCF earnings at LRMC were $5.0 million (excluding prescription drug costs).

Although AFMS plays an important role in support of the LRMC mission by contributing a significant portion of the military personnel that work at LRMC, it gets no recognition for their contribution to the workload. In addition, the Air Force AE squadron at Ramstein AB, less than 10 miles away, supports the LRMC mission by caring for patients from Europe and Southwest Asia while they are being transferred to and from LRMC.

Since AFMS will lose much of its inpatient capability as a result of FY 2005 BRAC decisions, the workload performed at LRMC will likely become increasingly important for maintaining currency. To meet its readiness missions, AFMS should consider increasing the Air Force presence at LRMC, as part of a strategy to maintain the currency of critical-care specialty staff. This is an example of the second option discussed in Chapter Six for expanding AFMS opportunities. LRMC could also provide additional leader development opportunities for AFMS personnel as a joint Army–Air Force organization. Increasing the focus on resources committed to LRMC, as well as on reporting and documenting these resources and the resulting workload, should be a priority concern for AFMS leadership, given the anticipated reductions in resources and military personnel staffing elsewhere. By highlighting LRMC's joint nature, AFMS's readiness need to maintain currency, and its efforts to support overseas medical requirements, AFMS can help justify staffing used to provide care at LRMC.

Bibliography

Air Force Surgeon General, "Who We Are," fact sheet, Official Web Site of the Air Force Surgeon General, undated. As of May 28, 2009:
http://www.sg.af.mil/factsheets/factsheet.asp?id=8182

American Association of Medical Colleges, web page. As of May 28, 2009:
http://www.aamc.org/advocacy/library/teachphys/phys0001.htm

Army Medical Department Center and School, *Department of Defense Medical Readiness Strategic Plan*, Ft. Sam Houston, Tex., March 20, 1995.

Bailey, Sue, "Policy to Improve Military Treatment Facility Primary Care Manager Enrollment Capacity," memorandum, Washington, D.C.: Office of the Secretary of Defense, Assistant Secretary of Defense for Health Affairs, March 6, 2000.

Base Realignment and Closure Commission, *Final Report*, September 8, 2005.

Bigelow, James H., Katherine M. Harris, and Richard Hillestad, *Measuring the Strategic Value of the Armed Forces Health Longitudinal Technology Application (AHLTA)*, Santa Monica, Calif.: RAND Corporation, MG-680-OSD, 2008. As of July 13, 2010:
http://www.rand.org/pubs/monographs/MG680/

BRAC—*See* Base Realignment and Closure Commission.

Brohi, Karim, "Injury Severity Score: Overview and Desktop Calculator," Trauma.org, March 10, 2007. As of July 13, 2010:
http://www.trauma.org/index.php/main/article/383/

CBO—*See* Congressional Budget Office.

Colarusso, Laura M., and Bryan Bender, "Pentagon Fears Healthcare Costs Will Erode Readiness—Aging Population Is Driving Up Fees," *Boston Globe*, March 5, 2007. As of May 28, 2009:
http://www.boston.com/news/nation/articles/2007/03/05/
pentagon_fears_healthcare_costs_will_erode_readiness/

Congressional Budget Office, *Restructuring Military Medical Care*, CBO Paper, Washington, D.C., July 1995.

———, "Growth in Medical Spending by the Department of Defense," Issue Brief, Washington, D.C., 2003.

Dahl, Peter E., "The Impact of the Establishment of the Defense Health Program Appropriation on the Planning, Programming, and Budgeting System Within the Department of Defense," Monterey, Calif.: Naval Postgraduate School, June 1993.

Davis, Susan, Statement of Chairwoman Susan Davis, U.S. House of Representatives, Military Personnel Subcommittee Hearing on the Future of Military Health Care, Washington, D.C.: U.S. Government Printing Office, 2008.

Defense Health Program, FY 2009 Budget Estimates, Appropriation Highlights, Exhibit PBA-19, undated.

Department of Defense 6015.1-M, "Glossary of Healthcare Terminology," manual, January 1999.

Department of Defense 6010.13-M, "Medical Expense and Performance Reporting System for Fixed Military Medical and Dental Treatment Facilities," manual, Washington, D.C.: Office of the Assistant Secretary of Defense, Health Affairs, April 7, 2008.

Department of Defense, Department of Defense Medical Readiness Strategic Plan (1995–2001), March 20, 1995.

———, "Fiscal Year 2005 Medicare Eligible Retiree Health Care Fund Audited Financial Statements," November 7, 2005. As of May 28, 2009:
http://comptroller.defense.gov/cfs/fy2005.html

Department of Defense Appropriations Bill, 2008, SR 110-155, January 4, 2007.

Department of Defense Directive 5136.01, Assistant Secretary of Defense for Health Affairs (ASD[HA]), Washington, D.C., June 4, 2008.

Department of Defense Instruction 6015.23, "Delivery of Healthcare at Military Treatment Facilities: Foreign Service Care; Third-Party Collection; Beneficiary Counseling and Assistance Coordinators," Washington, D.C.: Office of the Assistant Secretary of Defense, Health Affairs, October 30, 2002.

Eibner, Christine, *Maintaining Military Medical Skills During Peacetime: Outlining and Assessing a New Approach*, Santa Monica, Calif.: RAND Corporation, MG-638-OSD, 2008. As of July 13, 2010:
http://www.rand.org/pubs/monographs/MG638/

Escobar, Herb, "MEPRS Data Sources and Differences: EAS IV Repository vs. M2," briefing, Axiom Research Management, 2005. As of May 28, 2009:
http://www.meprs.info/dl.cfm?dl=05conf-13.ppt

Executive Order 9397, Numbering System for Federal Accounts Relating to Individual Persons, November 22, 1943.

Healthcare Cost and Utilization Project, "Overview of HCUP," website, last modified November 12, 2009. As of August 6, 2010:
http://www.hcup-us.ahrq.gov/overview.jsp

Hosek, Susan D., Joan Buchanan, and George A. Goldberg, *Reconciling Air Force Physicians' Peacetime and Wartime Capabilities: Demonstration of a Workforce Design Methodology*, Santa Monica, Calif.: RAND Corporation, R-3202-AF, 1985. As of July 13, 2010:
http://www.rand.org/pubs/reports/R3202/

Keating, Edward G., Marygail K. Brauner, Lionel A. Galway, Judith Mele, James J. Burks, and Brendan Saloner, *Air Force Physician and Dentist Multiyear Special Pay: Current Status and Potential Reforms*, Santa Monica, Calif.: RAND Corporation, MG-866-AF, 2009. As of July 13, 2010:
http://www.rand.org/pubs/monographs/MG866/

Keating, Edward G., Hugh G. Massey, Judith D. Mele, and Benjamin F. Mundell, *An Analysis of the Populations of the Air Force's Medical and Professional Officer Corps*, Santa Monica, Calif.: RAND Corporation, TR-782-AF, 2010. As of September 1, 2010:
http://www.rand.org/pubs/technical_reports/TR782/

Loftus, Thomas J., Assistant Surgeon General, Health Care Operations, "Defense Medical Human Resource System Internet (DMHRSi) Labor Cost Timesheet 100 Percent Compliance," memorandum, November 19, 2009.

MEPRS Manual—*See* Department of Defense, DoD 6010.13-M.

Murray, Mark, Mike Davies, and Barbara Boushon, "Panel Size: How Many Patients Can One Doctor Manage?" *Family Practice Management*, April 2007. As of May 28, 2009:
http://www.aafp.org/fpm/20070400/44pane.html

Program Budget Decision 742, December 14, 1991.

Singer, Neil M., Acting Assistant Director, National Security Division, Congressional Budget Office, testimony to the Subcommittee of Military Forces and Personnel, House Committee on the Armed Forces, Washington, D.C.: U.S. Government Printing Office, 1994.

Snyder, Don, Edward W. Chan, James J. Burks, Mahyar A. Amouzegar, and Adam C. Resnick, *How Should Air Force Expeditionary Medical Capabilities Be Expressed?* Santa Monica, Calif.: RAND Corporation, MG-785-AF, 2009. As of July 13, 2010:
http://www.rand.org/pubs/monographs/MG785/

U.S. Code, Title 10, Section 1079b, Procedures for Charging Fees for Care Provided to Civilians; Retention and Use of Fees Collected, January 3, 2007.

U.S. Code, Title 10, Section 1095, Health Care Services Incurred on Behalf of Covered Beneficiaries: Collection from Third-Party Payers, January 3, 2007.

U.S. General Accounting Office, *Medical Readiness: Efforts Are Underway for DoD Training in Civilian Trauma Centers*, Washington, D.C., GAO/NSIAD-98-75, April 1998.

Veterans Health Care Act of 1992, Public Law 102-585, November 4, 1992.

Yow, Mark, "History of the Military Treatment Facility 'Efficiency Wedge,'" Washington, D.C.: Office of the Secretary of Defense, Assistant Secretary of Defense for Health Affairs, paper, undated.